Praise for 'Mr. Zee Comes Home'

"In this deceptively simple little book Allan takes us on a complex journey, not only forcing the reader to fully confront their own position on life after death, but also taking us through the process of that confrontation. Any pet owner will be able to relate to the love expressed here, and to universal lessons about love that Allan clearly articulates. Allan's sense of humor makes this a very entertaining read.
~ **Duane and Catherine O'Kane,
Registered Clinical Counselors
Clearmind International Institute Inc.**

Intriguing! A beautiful love story.
~ **Samantha Perrin**

Allan K. Hunkin is "a lamplighter for our time"
~ **John Bradshaw, Author 'The Homecoming '**

Publisher Information

Published by Allan K. Hunkin
dba Equanimity Communications

For Editorial & Bulk Order contact

>MrZeeComesHome.com
>Suite 252 - 8623 Granville Street
>Vancouver Canada - V6P5A2

Website: MrZeeComesHome.com
Email: **MrZeeComesHome@gmail.com**

ISBN: 978-0-9918171-6-0 – First Published January 2014
V140302CS03 © 2014 Allan K. Hunkin

All contents copyright (c) 2013 MrZeeComesHome.com, Equanimity Communications and Allan Hunkin. All rights reserved. No part of this document or the related files may be reproduced or transmitted in any form, by any means (electronic, photocopying, recording, or otherwise) without the prior written permission of the publisher.

Links to Articles, Blogs and Websites: All information provided herein via links to Articles, Blogs and Websites remains the property of the original author and is provided here strictly for editorial purposes. For any additional information contact the authors, their blog or the website on which the piece was posted.

Limit of Liability and Disclaimer of Warranty: The publishing company has used its best efforts in preparing this book, and the information provided herein is provided 'as is.' MrZeeComesHome.com and/or Allan Hunkin make no representation or warranties with respect to the accuracy or completeness of the contents of this book, and specifically disclaim any implied warranties of merchantability or fitness for any particular purpose and shall in no event be liable for any loss of profit or any other commercial damage, including but not limited to special, incidental, consequential, or other damages.

Trademarks: This book identifies product names and services known to be trademarks, registered trademarks, or service marks of their respective holders. They are used throughout this book in an editorial fashion only. In addition, terms suspected of being trademarks, registered trademarks, or service marks have been appropriately capitalized, although MrZeeComesHome.com and Allan Hunkin cannot attest to the accuracy of this information.

Use of a term in this book should not be regarded as affecting the validity of any trademark, or service mark.

Declaration of integrity: If you have this file (or a printout) and didn't pay for it, you are depriving the author and publisher of their rightful royalties. Please make a donation at MrZeeComes Home.com. A portion of your declaration of integrity will be donated to a Charity chosen by the publisher.

Other books by Allan Hunkin:

Your Worthiness Cycle
Finding Better Solutions Faster
From Fire to Light

Join Allan and Mr. Zee on Social Networks

Facebook.com/mrzeecomeshome
Twitter - twitter.com/mrzeecomeshome
YouTube - youtube.com/mrzeecomeshome
LinkedIn – linkedin.com/in/allanhunkin

Speaking Engagements

To book Allan for radio and speaking engagements contact: Maureen Collins (**mrzeecomeshome@gmail.com**)

Dedication

This book is dedicated to everyone who is or has cared for a pet… and to the pets they love.

May you be visited with Peace every day for the rest of your life and beyond.

Words of Gratitude and Appreciation

Thank you to Judy Yates, not only for your many contributions and edits, but for providing safe haven so I could focus on telling this story without interruption.

Thank you Shelora Fitzgerald, for your inspiration, encouragement and continued belief in me and my work. I am deeply grateful for our many conversations. Your suggestions, edits and your dedication to telling this story in the clearest way possible is on every page of this book.

Thank you to Tanis for loving Miss Zulu back to life, and finding us Mr. Zee so the four of us could love each other as much as we knew how to love at the time.

Thank you to Dan and Marzia Molatore and Rob Rivers for your friendship and support through some very rough times, including the death of our friend Mr. Zee.

Thank you to my son Larry for being the extraordinary human being that you are.

Thank you to all my teachers throughout the years, especially Zig Ziglar, Dr. Chuck Spezzano and John Bradshaw for lifting me high enough to be able to have these extraordinary experiences.

Finally, I want to thank David and Lorinda Rawlings for your support and sponsorship of this project and others.

About Allan Hunkin

Allan is a life enrichment speaker, writer, broadcaster who has been involved in the personal growth and empowerment field for over thirty years.

In addition, Allan has experience in such diverse fields as Farming, Manufacturing, Airshow Management, Flying, Business Consulting and Life Coaching.

From 1979 to 1990 Allan was involved in the sport aircraft industry, first as a dealer, then as a manufacturer, and finally as a senior sales and marketing executive. His flying career included flight testing new designs of light aircraft, and performing at airshows across North America. In 1985, Allan was chosen as Flight Leader of the six plane formation team *'The Northern Lights.'*

In 1994, Allan began to research and develop a unique approach to understanding the dynamic cycles of self-esteem, self worth and self acceptance. He calls this new hybrid model, "The Worthiness Cycle." Allan has written extensively and delivered many seminars on this subject.

Beginning in 1997, Allan began hosting his own radio show. Since that time he has conducted over 700 radio interviews with authors, thought leaders and change agents from around the world.

From 1999 to 2004 Allan was president of the "SuccessTALK Channels," an online broadcasting company that hosted over two hundred Internet radio programs. He is the author of four books:

> *Mr. Zee Comes Home*
> *Your Worthiness Cycle*
> *Finding Better Solutions Faster*
> *From Fire to Light (Screenplay)*

Allan lives in Vancouver, Canada.

Table of Contents

Other books by Allan Hunkin: _____ 3
Join Allan and Mr. Zee on Social Networks _____ 3
Speaking Engagements _____ 3
Dedication _____ 4
Words of Appreciation _____ 4
Introduction _____ 9
Not a Good Time to Write This Book _____ 10
My Hidden Agenda _____ 13
Introducing Mr. Zee _____ 14
Part I - Call The Paramedics _____ 15
July 17, 2010 – The Moment Everything Changes _____ 15
Fleeting Flashes of Light _____ 25
Part II - The First Encounters _____ 27
Late July 2010 - "Holy Kitty Litter, The Covers Are Moving!" _27
The Clash of Our Two Minds _____ 30
The Second Visit _____ 31
Fall 2012 - Too Busy Living to Notice What is Real _____ 34
Part III – Being Blessed With Zulu and Mr. Zee _____ 37
Fall 1998 - A Princess Arrives _____ 37
The Walking Hair Ball _____ 44
Saving Our Princess _____ 45
Part IV – The King and I _____ 49
Summer 2005 - Two Bachelors in Marpole _____ 49
The Zen of Scratch _____ 57
Part V - The Whole Game Changes _____ 63
January 2013 - Am I Going Nuts? _____ 63

Many Questions _____ 64
Part VI - Movements, Sensations and Feelings _____ 67
I *'Must'* Be Able to See Something _____ 72
Part VII - The Four Mouseketeers _____ 77
Spring 2013 - Gina's Place _____ 77
Summer 2013 - The RV Park _____ 80
October 30, 2013 - All Night Long _____ 82
October 31, 2013 - The Two Z's _____ 84
Looking For Patterns _____ 86
Part VIII – More Extraordinary Every Day _____ 87
December 9th – Sharing Energy _____ 87
Hey, There's An App For That _____ 93
Seeing Really is Believing _____ 94
First Sighting _____ 95
Part IX – Back To The Future _____ 97
Past Experiences _____ 97
Understanding Belief _____ 107
Part X - Worthiness: The Key To Everything _____ 111
Worthiness Explained _____ 113
Worthiness IS The Gateway to Everything _____ 116
Stay Tuned. This Adventure Continues _____ 119
In Conclusion (for now) _____ 119
What Have I Learned? _____ 119
Appendix _____ 123
Chronological Order of Events and Happening _____ 123
Pets Coming Back Research _____ 128
Pictures of Cats That Have Appeared in Photographs _____ 129

Sometimes, you find yourself in the middle of nowhere, and sometimes, in the middle of nowhere, you find yourself.

Introduction

> *"You want to know whether I believe in ghosts. Of course I do not believe in them. If you had known as many of them as I have, you would not believe in them either."*
> ~ **Don Marqui**

Almost everybody who has had a real life encounter with a spirit or ghost starts out telling their story in the same way: "*I've never believed in Ghosts.*" Then, inevitably, they go on to tell you what happened that changed their mind forever.

This is not really a book about ghosts. But, until you have more of the context of the story, 'ghosts' is the best word I can use.

This is a story about a real life man (me) and a real life cat named Mr. Zee. Nothing special about that. As far as I know, I am very much alive, and Mr. Zee is not, at least not in the *"chowing down in his bowl, eating grub I bought at Safeway"* kind of way.

I lost Mr. Zee too early for my liking. He had lived a good life and his death was mercifully unexpected and quick. I consoled myself by saying he was in his senior years, so he would not have been around forever. At least that is what I thought at the time.

What happened, both at the time of his death and since, has challenged me to my core and altered my construct of reality.

Although I was not officially a 'believer' in a religious way. I have never had much of a problem with the idea of 'spirit beings.' I had no real '*proof*' but I was just slightly more inclined to believe in their existence than not. Who cares really? As long as they were not scaring the living daylights out of my family, or devaluing property values in the neighborhood, it didn't much matter to me.

Having spent thirty plus years involved in self-help and personal empowerment, you would think my approach to life would be mostly progressive and open-minded. Not true about me, at least not right now. I am grouchy and not overly impressed with human beings at the moment. I am more inclined to be cynical when presented with something new, unexpected, or out of the norm.

While it is true that I have been exposed to many teachings that have expanded my awareness of an inner and outer life, I still have as much trouble as anyone when suspending disbelief is required.

We all share some common fears. We fear if we reveal any unusual experiences to others, we will be labeled insane, kooky, or at the very least a 'little strange.' This fear is fueled by one of the deepest anxieties we have as human beings, the terror of being ostracized and abandoned by family, friends and community. In reading this book, I encourage you not to let these natural fears get in the way of a balanced investigation of the facts as I present them.

Nothing in this book is intended to frighten you. If I startle you, and you put this book down, never to pick it up again, I have failed in telling this true story in palatable bits that you were able to digest.

Not a Good Time to Write This Book

I did not want to write this book, at least not at this time. I steadfastly resisted the idea for more than a year.

I was very involved in producing a new seminar on Worthiness, based upon research I have been engaged in since 1994. For several reasons, I was under pressure to publish what I had learned and time was of the essence.

However, come the fall of 2013, I simply could resist no longer. The extraordinary happenings and experiences were simply too compelling, and too important for me, and for us, as human beings, to ignore.

The first part of *'Mr. Zee Comes Home'* is written from memory. Memory is enough however; because the initial experiences were so 'unbelievable' that they are indelibly imprinted on my mind.

The latter parts, since has been written in real time. The happenings, as recounted in this book, continue and when they will stop (if ever) is unknown.

"Physics changes, but reality stays the same."
~ **Richard Bandler, Co-founder**
Neuro-Linguistic Programming

I love stories. As a writer and professional speaker, I am naturally an enthusiastic storyteller. In articles, blog posts, and books that I've previously written I've often taken 'poetic license' to more effectively make a point, or make the telling of the story more clear and/or enjoyable to read.

Not in this case. Throughout the writing of this book, I have been dedicated to not modifying, expanding, or embellishing this recounting in any way. I sought the assistance of professionals and friends alike to help me identify any folklore, urban myth or 'BS' that had seeped in. As a result, this book is as truthful and accurate as I know how to make.

Another reason I was reluctant to write this book was that I did not really feel qualified.

I grew up on a farm in rural Manitoba and my 'red-neck' background still seeps out every once in a while. Although we went to church every Sunday, religion was not at the center of our family life. I rejected religion early in my life, something that continues to this day. Although I expose myself to the teachings of many, I am committed to no one teacher in particular.

I have been involved in self-help, both for my personal growth and professionally, for many years but I have not pursed the deeper aspects of spirituality. Oh, I nibbled around the edges, but I never allowed myself to just fall into the deep end of the pool, and stay there.

Do we have a soul? Is there life after death? Can we come back after we die? What and where is the place we come back from? Do we have angels and guides around us at times, assisting us through life? Do they need our permission, or are they doing things without our permission? I had no 'earthly idea' of how to answer these questions.

If you had pinned me in a corner, and would not let me avoid giving you an answer, I would have been inclined towards the negative response. "No. We do not' live again.

I have plenty of friends who are involved in the deeper aspects of spirituality. Often, in order to fit in, I *'appeared'* to be spiritual, but to be truthful, I secretly felt a bit superior. I did not really 'buy in' and I certainly was not going to allow myself to be hooked by all the *'booga booga.'* Life was already complicated enough, without adding something that no one could really prove. In this vein, a number of years ago, I wrote an article in the local 'empowerment' monthly entitled:

> ***"If Spiritually is Really the Way To Go, How Come it's So Damned Hard to Pay The Rent?"***

I have done some really dumb things in my life. As a result, I carry some regret, shame, guilt and fear mixed in with the good stuff.

All of this to say that the reasons I've experienced the things I have written about in this book is not because I have a more direct path to the Divine. I do not claim to have an overly innocent mind. I am not psychic, clairvoyant or 'clair' anything, at least no more than anyone else.

I am not seeking enlightenment consciously, and would probably run away from it if it stood in front of me on the sidewalk.

I have been setting myself up to live a pretty simple life in my senior years. I intend to write a few screenplays, novels, and self-help books, put on some seminars, and possibly re-launch my radio show. My goal is to live full time in my motorhome, travelling south for the winter, and north once it gets warm. I had nothing to prove, when all this began, and I still don't. I was not seeking an exciting story to tell, or to create anything significant at all.

This is why, when Mr. Zee came back the first few times, I didn't make a big deal out of it. Sure, it was cool, but I was busy, too busy to give it much mind. I did not stop to think about it much because, if I did, I suspected it was going to get in the way of my plans to live out my years in a quiet, calm, low-key manner.

That was the plan. Then, Mr. Zee came back again, this time in full force, and I realized the ramifications of his visits are just too relevant to the times we live in to ignore.

I realize that this is a rather long introduction but I feel it is important for you to know what was going on in my head, before you invest the time to read this book.

Do we live on? You are the only one that can decide that, no matter how much others try to influence you. All you can do is to honestly and objectively invest in becoming more aware of 'maybe.'

My Hidden Agenda

My agenda in writing this book has been to '*have no agenda*', other than to inform, educate, and entertain.

Well, that is not quite true. Rather than an agenda, I have a 'wish.' My wish is that, in reading this book your understanding and awareness of things not normally experienced is expanded, and your life is enhanced as a result.

I am not selling anything designed to alter your perceptions. I am not out to save your soul, or have you join a church, cult, or even an animal rescue society or service club.

And, no, I am not a member of "The Illuminati."

However, an invitation is always extended for you to join a group of us every year at the Super Bowl, where we run around naked and chant to our god whom we call 'Bud' because he's wiser.

Yes, as a result of reading this book, your perceptions might change in some way, but not because I have invested any of my mind time in deliberately causing that to happen.

So, do not take my word for it. Investigate everything you read here for yourself. Keep what fits for you, and let the rest fall where it may. I encourage you to be skeptical. But remember, a true skeptic also '*doubts their doubt.*'

There are likely to be some who will say I did this to make a lot of money. To that I say, *"I certainly hope so."* But, they should also be aware that the "He's a kook," factor is likely to cost me customers and credibility in my day job. This whole 'cat dies and comes back' story could just as easily turn out to be a net loss as well.

I don't know, and I personally don't much care either, if some people reject this story as mere fantasy. I feel that the information contained here could be too important to the evolution of our overall consciousness. to worry about such things.

Besides, Mr. Zee would likely say that keeping this information a secret would not be nearly as much fun as the havoc it's going to generate in some people's minds.

Introducing Mr. Zee

My friend, confidant and Guru, well, sometimes my Guru, except when he is waking me up at four o'clock in the morning.

Part I - Call The Paramedics

July 17, 2010 – The Moment Everything Changes

"Oh my god... I'm dying!"

About 2:00 am, from a deep sleep I suddenly shot straight up in bed.

My heart was pounding so hard I thought it was going to burst out of my chest. My head was enveloped in excruciating pain.

The first thought I can remember was "I must be having both a heart attack and a stroke at the same time!"

In a panic I struggled to call out to my roommate who was sleeping in the bedroom across the hall. No words or sounds came. I tried again, but quickly gave up. "Maybe I can just breathe my way through it," I told myself. As hard as it was, I concentrated on taking slow, deep breaths, trying to get my heart rate down. I calculated that was probably my only chance of surviving.

After about thirty seconds, the pain began to subside, and within a minute or so, it was gone completely.

I sat there for a few minutes, my heart and my mind racing, wondering, *"What the hell just happened?* What could cause such intense pain in both my head and my heart simultaneously? Had I been dreaming? Was it just a nightmare? Had I bumped my head on the wall or something? I had just switched medications for a condition I have. Could that be the problem? Was there something wrong with me? I had never experienced anything like it before, nor had I ever heard of anyone else having anything similar happen to them.

I exhausted all the possibilities in my mind. Everything quickly returned to normal. A few minutes later, I lay back down and was soon asleep.

The next morning, I felt fine. There was no hint of the intense pain I had experienced in the middle of the night. Other than making a note to ask my doctor about side effects, I did not give it much further thought.

I looked around for Mr. Zee. There was still a bit of food left in his food dish. I assumed he must have stayed out all night 'tom cattin,' as my dad use to say when I hadn't come home at nights.

Staying out was not unusual for Mr. Zee. He had been an outdoor cat for the entire eleven years we had been together. I always left a window ajar for him so he could come and go as he pleased.

My apartment in Marpole where Mr. Zee and I lived

A few years earlier that choice had cost me a wide screen TV. Someone had broken in through Mr. Zee's open window, unlocked the door to my apartment from the inside, and simply walked out with it. That was a big 'ouch.' At that time, a wide screen TV cost around $3000, and I had not finished paying for it yet. But, Mr. Zee was my 'bud,' so I gritted my teeth, and swallowed the loss.

I did start to wonder when he didn't show up by the second night. That had only happened once before that I could recall.

The next morning, I extended my daily walk around the neighborhood just to see if I could catch sight of him, but nothing. I was not too worried. He could look after himself.

The Knock at the Door

The next afternoon I heard a timid knock at my door. Opening it, I did not recognize either the man or woman standing there.

"Hello. We live up stairs," they explained. "Do you have a white cat?"

"Yes. I do." At this point, I'm thinking, "Mr. Zee, you little bugger, finding your way into someone else's apartment 'again' for some extra chow!"

"We're very sorry to tell you this, but he was killed two nights ago. It has taken until now for us to find out who might be his master.

We're so sorry!"

With that, tears started to do what tears do on both their faces.

Stumbling for something to say, I asked, "What happened?"

They both looked at each other and I saw their faces turn from sadness to horror. The woman spoke with her head down, as if not wanting to re-live the memory.

"Two coyote's chased him. They both grabbed onto him at the same time."

Not actually talking to me, she said looking off into the distance "Awful!"

"Where did it happen?" I asked.

"In the park across the street, by the cement bench. We saw the whole thing."

Trying to console me, the woman told me it was all over in seconds.

"We love cats. We're so sorry for your loss."

I thanked them for taking the time to locate and telling me, and then slowly closed the door. I found the closest chair and sat down, hard.

I cringed as my mind raced back to a poster I had seen on a telephone pole right outside my apartment.

I immediately jumped head first into blaming myself.

> **WARNING**
> Keep your pets inside. Coyotes have been spotted in the neighborhood.

I had not been paying attention. Mr. Zee had been so fast and frisky for so many years that I had just never considered the possibility that he was vulnerable.

"God damn it" I thought to myself. "Why am I always so bloody busy that I miss important things like this? I have failed Mr. Zee... again!"

Blame is easier to feel than the intense pain of grief and loss.

I was paralyzed.

Later that day I contacted friends and family with calls and emails letting them know what had happened. Within a few hours, friends

A view of the park across the street where
Mr. Zee encountered the coyote

started showing up on my doorstep, some of them in tears. It seems I was not the only one who loved my little white buddy.

Trying to Cry

As with any sudden death in a family, it takes a day or so for it to sink in. I was dazed, walking around in a fog. Nothing seemed real. I ran instant replay's of his horrible death over and over in my mind. Using denial along with a leap in logic, I felt sure that I was going to wake up from this terrible nightmare shortly.

I have always had trouble crying. I had not cried for either of my parents when they died. I had lost several friends early in my life from farm accidents and reckless driving. Later on, in my 30's, while in the high-risk business of airshow flying, I had lost several of my close flying buddies. Even with those close friends, I did not cry. For some unknown reason I have a mind that becomes calm and clear in the middle of a crisis.

I am not a religious man, so it was not that I believed *"He's up in Heaven. He is in a better place. He's in God's hands now."* I had always tried to avoid saying those kinds of things, the trite words we say to try to console others and ourselves in the face of death.

The morning after I got the news, I knew, this time, it had to be different. Denial was not an option. If I were to be true to myself and to the love I had for this guy who had made his way so deeply into my heart, I would have to allow myself to cry.

I made my way over to the spot in the park where the neighbors had said he has lost the race to live.

I thought, maybe if I just sit on this bench, I will be able to find the tears that, yet again, seemed unwilling to help me release the growing pain, grief and guilt.

Mr. Zee is Dead and It's All MY FAULT!

To most everyone else it must have seemed like I was a pretty good master, but I knew that I had made some really bad mistakes that had caused Mr. Zee a lot of pain and almost killed him more than once.

Mr. Zee was a long-haired cat. He had to constantly lick his coat to keep it clean. Being able to go outside whenever he wanted to, I did not notice that he had completely stopped using his litter.

I didn't realize that his lower intestine had gotten completely impacted with hair and undigested food. This happened three times, and I wish I could say it was from natural causes but it was not. I simply hadn't been careful enough. I had been told by the Vet what I needed to do: feed him only soft (more expensive) food, get his hair shaved in the summer time so he wouldn't have so much to clean, and add a little mineral oil to his food each day, so that everything would move through more easily.

I did do what I was instructed, but for one reason or another, I did not do any of those things consistently.

It has been said that, *"The way you do anything in life is the way you do everything."* That was certainly true for me; the story of my life, not consistently doing the things I knew needed to be done to avoid problems, or doing the things necessary to be safe and successful. In short, I was somewhat of a reckless risk taker who often figured the rules did not really apply to me.

Zee had his third painful episode about four months before he was killed. As a result, I was having to shoot a laxative into his mouth both in the morning and at night, which, this time, I was doing consistently Neither of us liked the process, but we had gotten used to it, and he was gaining strength. But the recurrence of the condition that had I allowed to develop over time had weakened and slowed him down. I never considered that he would be unable to run to safety as quickly as he could have previously.

At the time of his death, I was carrying around a lot of guilt about my self-centeredness. Some residue guilt still resides within me.

Holding On

Sitting on the bench, my mind could not bear any more pain. I stood up and headed back to my apartment. Suddenly, I noticed some-thing lying just under the edge of the bench I had been sitting on.

It was a paw, a white paw with a bit of bone left on the end of it.

Oh god, this is all that's left of my beloved friend," I said aloud.

I sat back down, and the tears finally began streaming from my eyes. I had killed him with my stupidity and neglect, and nothing was ever going to change that.

I went back to the apartment, got a plastic zip lock bag, retrieved the paw and put it in my freezer.

"Mr. Zee will be with me for ever" I thought. Having part of him will help me cope with the pain."

The crying stopped. The pain subsided. A couple of months later I discarded the paw. The guilt remained.

Grief Showing Up As Anger

As a counselor I had recommended to clients to use the grief to cleanse themselves of all regrets and loss they were carrying around, not only from their most recent loss but from all past losses as well. I should have followed my own advice and just stayed in the sadness and let grief run its natural course. Instead, I did what many people do. I got mad as hell.

"I'm going to kill that 'fu**ing' coyote, and force his partner to watch!" became the dominant thought running around in my head.

Coyotes hunt at night. Later that evening I got dressed up in black, for camouflage, and went out in search of the 'son of a bitch; that took my Mr. Zee away from me.

A Course in Miracles (ACIM) says that 'Guilt always spurs attack.' On the surface, it might seem like I was seeking revenge. But really, my actions were being fueled by the guilt I felt for not looking after Mr. Zee as well as I could have.

I walked the neighborhood from midnight until about 5:00 am, equipped only with a baseball bat. My plan was to get close enough to bash one of the coyote's brains in, and then hang it from a tree in the park for all the other coyotes to get the message.

The next morning I told my roommate, Rob, what I was thinking about doing. (I didn't want him to know that I had already been out all night. He might think I had flipped my lid.)

As gently as he could, Rob suggested that maybe I wasn't thinking very clearly. That was true. But then again, that fact had never stopped me from doing a lot of dumb things before.

Rob indicated that he didn't really approve, but, as a Doctorial student at the University of British Columba, he would do what he could to help. He first headed to his computer to research coyotes and their characteristics.

Rob reported back to me later that day that Coyotes hunt at a saunter of about 12-14 miles an hour and can gust up to 45 mph if sufficiently motivated. They don't actually hunt their prey, as much as they just arrive unexpectedly out of the blue, and take advantage of the surprise.

I realized that if I were going to kill this bastard, I would need a gun. Growing up on a farm, I had done some hunting. As a kid, I had been fascinated with guns, and was a pretty good shot given that my vision in one eye has not been good since birth. However, hauling a high powered rifle around my neighborhood at night didn't seem like a very good idea, unless I wanted to attract a bunch of squad cars and cops yelling "Get on the ground and put the gun down or we'll shoot!"

That afternoon I arranged to meet a guy at a local coffee shop who knew 'people' that would sell you a handgun with no questions asked. Rifles are fairly easy to obtain in Canada, but handguns are strictly controlled.

As we huddled over a cup of coffee, he suggested I get a legal CO2 pellet pistol. "They are high powered enough to kill an animal, but they don't make enough noise to startle the neighbors" he said, smiling only slightly. "Don't buy it through a local store," he told me. "Pellet gun or not, if you kill somebody you're still going away for a few years."

"Get me one," I instructed him, "the strongest one you can. I don't care what it costs."

"Sure, and we never met... right?" he said, giving me a look that convinced me, in no uncertain terms, that we had never met.

I nodded. He nodded. Coffee break was over.

Still carrying my bat, I headed out that night. Thanks to Rob, I knew more about what I was up against.

No glimpse of him that night or the next. On the fourth night, I caught sight of a coyote a block away, running at their normal pace.

I ran like hell up a back alley, hoping to meet him face to face when he rounded the corner. Reaching the end of the block, I leaned up close against a corner building, and drew my bat from under my coat. I was up wind of him, so he wouldn't smell me until it was too late. "Finally! Retribution at last!"

After what seemed like a long minute, I poked my head around the corner of the building to see how close he was getting. No bloody coyote anywhere in sight.

"Damn, he must have turned the other direction," I cursed under my breath. I hurried out into the middle of the street to see if I could catch sight of him and plan for a second attack, but he had vanished.

I continued my nightly hunts. Sleep became elusive. Throughout the day, I walked the neighborhood, talking to neighbors, trying to locate where the coyotes were hanging out. I still wanted this guy bad, and I was going to get him.

Many people reported sightings but I never got a single glimpse of him again. Over the next couple of months cat disappearances in the neighborhood subsided, probably because they had killed most of the outdoor cats. It was estimated that they had killed more than thirty cats in the Marpole neighborhood. I was only one of many who were nursing a broken heart.

Forgiveness Seeps In

By the fifth night, I was starting to calm down and get control of my rage. They were coyotes after all, doing what coyotes do. They had been starving where they were living before, and only wanted to feed their own 'beloved' offspring.

I know only too well what it's like to be hungry. I married very young. As a new husband and father, I needed a paycheck every week to feed those whom I had become responsible for. At such a young age, however, I hadn't really figured out how to feed myself yet, let alone feed a family. Having no higher education and a very high powered Type A personality (code for hyper-active ADHD) I had to take jobs selling, which I always struggled at. Under pressure to 'bring home the bacon,' I found myself having to sell things I didn't really believe in, to people who didn't really need or want what I was selling. Adding to that I had decided that booze was the best way to sooth my inner demons. Along with booze came parties and along with parties came women. You get my drift I'm sure.

Maybe if my past had been squeaky clean, I would have continued pursuing retribution. But, after some introspection, I realized that it was mostly my guilt of the past that was fueling my actions in the present. It was time to let it go of <u>both</u>, the guilt, and the current behaviors that had resulted from it.

I think many times we experience people (and ourselves) as very angry. I bet, if we were to dig deep enough, we would find that disappointment, heartbreak, grief and loss is actually at the core, fueling their hostile attitude and behavior. I wish I had learned earlier that responding with compassion, rather than reciprocating with anger is *'always'* the answer.

Once my vendetta had run its course, over the two weeks that followed, I began to accept what had happened, and what I had experienced. A serious reality check from the heart was due.

Mr. Zee had lived a good long life.. He had been loved by many. By most measurements it was a life well lived, He was sick, and old. Instead of lingering, he had a mercifully quick death. We should all be so fortunate!

Fleeting Flashes of Light

"Ghosts only exist for those who wish to see them."
~ Holtei

It was not to long afterwards that I started to see things flash in my peripheral vision. There were several times but I remember specifically once, in my apartment, I thought saw something move around the corner into the kitchen, more or less in the direction of where Mr. Zee's food bowl had been located.

A few days later, outside the apartment, something went very fast around the corner of the building before I could see what it was. Both times caused me to do a double take. I was convinced that what had moved was white.

"Maybe it's the ghost of Mr. Zee," I joked to myself, with no real commitment to the idea. Like many people, I dismissed the idea as being only a wishful hope coming to the surface from my suppressed sadness and remorse.

Finally, acceptance of what had happened, and forgiveness for my part in it, allowed me to climb back into my life and start to be productive again. Being overly absorbed in work helped the grief and sadness to fade. Painful thoughts of losing Mr. Zee throughout the day began to subside. The feelings of his presence dissipated. I did have a few flashes of him in my dreams, smiling at me, but nothing so vivid that it followed me after I woke.

It is within this context of routine, everyday living, that what happened next was so startling and profound.

Part II - The First Encounters

Late July 2010 - "Holy Kitty Litter, The Covers Are Moving!"

"The Supernatural is the Natural, just not yet understood."
~ Elbert Hubbard

Just over two weeks after Mr. Zee's departure, at about 10:30 pm, I was doing something I rarely do. I was sitting up in bed, reading. I don't remember what book it was, but I do remember I was sort of half reading, and half gazing at the end of the bed thinking about other stuff.

Suddenly, I felt something familiar, something that I had experienced hundreds of times before. There was the initial hop and landing on the mattress, followed by the deliberate, pacing around my legs in search of the perfect spot, followed by the customary 'flop' against the outside of my right leg in preparation for a quick wash, and then a long snooze.

I looked down to where the sensation was coming from.

With each step, I could see a corresponding indentation made by an invisible paw pushing down on the top blanket. When he flopped It only took a second or two for me to realize what was happening.

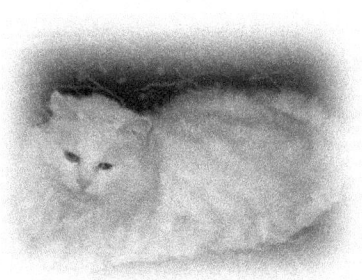

Although I hadn't spent a lot time learning about things paranormal, his presence was unmistakable. Mr. Zee had come to visit with me, and was currently sitting on our bed

An instant freight ran through my entire body. It took me thirty seconds or so to be able to jump back 'into' my body. I blurted out:

"Holy Shit, Mr. Zee! You scared the "Living Begeevers" out of me!"

It is amazing how fast our mind works in trying to make sense of what is happening, so it can give us what we need to survive the unknown, and un-expected. In an instant I was reminded of something I had read about Sprits returning. It seems that when someone dies a quick, violent death, their spirit sometimes comes back to reassure a loved one that they are OK. I had never really believed this before but here it was so I might as well go with the flow and see what happens. After getting over the initial shock, I realized I was certainly glad to 'see' him.

"How are you buddy? Are you OK?" I asked in a happy tone, trying not to sound too surprised or frightened.

There was no direct response, but I got a sense that he was letting me know that there was nothing to be afraid of.

"Great to have you back Zee I have missed you very much." I said with overwhelming emotion rising from my heart.

Then I thought, "That's silly. Why would I miss him? He is right here." He wasn't 'in the flesh,' so to speak, but I had no doubt whatsoever that he was, in fact, really with me now.

I had also read that it takes a lot of energy for a Spirit to re-manifest enough physically for us to recognize and experience their presence as real. What a guy! Mr. Zee had made the effort to come back, not for himself, but for my benefit.

"Wow" I said, *"I'm so honored. Thank you, 'Zee Man,' for coming back to let me know you're OK. I know it is taking a lot for you to do this."*

While I am speaking to Zee in a friendly relaxed tone, Inside I am beginning to feel anything but. Suppressed memories of all the Hollywood and TV horror films I watched as a kid were starting to fuel my fears. "What if it's really Freddy Krueger, or Dracula or the Amityville Ghosts? What if I'm about to be 'possessed?" I was quickly becoming overwhelmed with fear of the unknown. After all, in 30 seconds, I had gone from, not really being a 'believer,' to feeling a , a warm, body, strangely akin to that of my beloved cat, on curled up next to my leg!

Putting a brave face on it, I continued speaking: *"It's great that you came back to see me, but you don't need to stay any longer. I will be OK. You can go into the Light now, if you want."*

> *"The ghosts you chase you never catch."*
> JOHN MALKOVICH, London *Independent,* Apr. 5, 1992

Having said that, I realized I didn't really want him to go. My loneliness had reignited the need to have him back in this world with me.

As humans, when we have a heightened experience of love, we want more. We make a grab for it, attempting to hold on. Ironically, as that longing to keep him at my side came into my heart, Mr. Zee's presence began to fade. Within a few seconds, he was no longer with me. My personality protection mechanism, (otherwise known as my ego) kicked in, and I instantly felt alone and afraid.

It took a few minutes for my heart rate to settle down. The excitement along with the stress and the need to consciously respond beyond my beliefs had really drained me. I fell asleep quickly, and had no dreams, pleasant or otherwise, that I recall.

We Live Forever. So What! Back to Work.

The next morning, after having one of the most profound experiences that any human being can have, I did what many 'normal' people would do. I allowed my mind to convince me that it had not been real, or at the very least, was not as real as I was remembering it now.

I had been given the answer to the most fundamental question that every human being asks. "Do we survive death?" But, now doubt was seeping in.

Mr. Zee had answered that question simply by hopping on to my bed, just as he had done so many times before. The only difference was that, this time, without any question in my mind, he was *dead* when he did it!

His visit had offered me some proof that movies like 'Ghost,' 'Powder,' and 'Always,' were likely based much more on fact, than Mythology. And, if those movies were true, it would not be much of a stretch to believe that many other things 'unseen' and not easily proven are also true.

I am blessed with a mind that see's things in 3D. In an instant it began showing me a matrix that connected a lot of the dots.

Seeing this expanded vision allowed my 'higher' mind to reveal a few leaps in logic that my rational mind would never have made on it's own... "If Spirits can manifest themselves whenever they want, then it is also true that we can, in fact, manifest anything we want. And, if that's true, then hard work, education, and having been 'born on the right side of the tracks' has much less to do with our achievements, success and fulfillments than we have been giving them credit for.

This answers why those holding power in the world want to seed and fertilize the doubt and fear and disconnection we experience in life. Seeing what I was seeing in my mind nobody would ever work as hard ever again because they would understand how principles like the Law of Attraction work and make them a central and guiding principle in their lives.

The Clash of Our Two Minds

As interesting and exciting as my 'inspired' mind is, my logical mind is often stronger and more powerful, at least in moments when I'm not paying attention. My major challenge in life has been living with these two powerful minds and giving over way to much power to my logical mind.

You would think this time would have been different. In spite of overwhelming evidence to the contrary, delivered with tender care by a being I loved and trusted, I allowed my logical mind to have it's way with me again.

I let the opportunity to learn this key lesson slip away and headed at the speed of racing charge cards, right back into the life of struggle I was so familiar with, and seemingly committed to holding on to.

How many times do similar experiences happen to us, and we either dismiss them outright as delusionary, or else pay them little attention? How often does a book seem to fall off the shelf right in front of us, the perfect book with the perfect message for us at this particular time in our lives, and we ignore it? How often do we have a chat at a coffee shop with a complete stranger, and they seem to know exactly what to say to help us through something? If you never see that person again how do you know that they were actually a 'real' person?"

Have you ever had a dream where someone was in the room with you speaking to you? Have you wondered if they were actually there or just a dream? Science and psychology have provided answers but, for some reason, they always seem to fall short of the answer that would put the matter to rest.

However, none of this mattered at all at that time. With all the financial pressures, commitments, time constraints I was working with, I didn't have time to dilly-dally or ponder what all of this meant. Instead, I relegated this extraordinary and profound experience to a not often visited corner of my mind.

The Second Visit

> *"Unconditional love is without beginning or end, exists everywhere and found nowhere, is never proven yet instantly known."*
> ~ **Harold W. Becker**

Mr. Zee must have been watching me do the preverbal SSDD ("Same Shit, Different Day") and decided he had to hit me over the head with the facts, only harder, if I was ever going to 'get it.'

He waited one night to see if I would 'wake up' from the doubt and delusions I was enveloped in. I didn't. Zee returned the third night for a refresher course called 'Reality Worth Paying Attention To.'

I had just climbed into bed and had turned over to fluff my pillow when I felt the now famous, 'hop and plop' maneuver, once again. I turned back over and sat up so I was looking towards where it seemed he had landed. I felt him walk for half a dozen steps to his favorite spot. This time, however, the covers were not moving as he walked.

"He must be getting lighter," I explained to myself.

My ego immediately went into protection mode. Even though I had already experienced a visit from Zee, during which nothing evil, scary or dangerous had happened, I became frightened.

I mean, once could have been a fluke,. Who knew? Maybe it was just indigestion, or possibly even a hallucination. However, two visits in three days is pretty hard to glaze over, even for a confirmed fence sitter like myself. I took a moment to gain some control of my better self.

"Hello again my friend," I said. "It seems you are getting lighter. What are you doing back here so soon?"

Regardless of my enlightened responses, he was probably pretty sure I had not really understood the significance of his first visit. Being ever the gentleman Mr. Zee was kind enough not to give any indication of something he had suspected for years... namely that I was dumb as a bag of hammers and barely worth the effort as a student of his 'How Everything Works' Course.'

As much as I wanted my buddy's loving warmth lying on my chest again, I felt that it was not fair for me to be in the way of Mr. Zee's next step in his transformation.

> (Hey, I'm no dummy you know. I watched several episodes of 'Touched By An Angel' and knew that Zee needed to go with the star of the show into the light from whence he came.)

I took a minute to consider the best way to say what I felt I needed to be said.

"Mr. Zee, you are such a pal. Thank you for coming to see me again. I know you are concerned about me, but it's OK. I'm fine. and now, thanks to your visits, I know you are fine as well."

> (Actually I was concerned that he might have been confused and didn't know what he needed to do next.)

"As much as I am happy you have come back to visit me, I want you to know that it is time to set us both free from any obligations we might feel to each other. I feel it is time for you to rise above this 'in between realm' and go into the Light."

> (As the theory goes, Spirits who are killed quickly often don't actually realize that they are dead. They are stuck, with not quite enough energy to rise into the Light themselves.)

I had no way of telling but if this was the case but I wanted to help Mr. Zee make his 'transition.' But, I really had no idea what I could do to help him do that. I grabbed at what I had seen as a child. I prayed to God in Heaven.

"Dear God. Thank you for Mr. Zee and all his love. Please welcome him into Heaven."

Then I remembered a guided mediation that my friend Chuck Spezzano (Spezzano) had given in one of his workshops. Closing my eyes, I located 'my own 'inner light.' I visualized myself enveloping Mr. Zee in the light of this loving energy. Then I visualized us melting into just the one bright Light. Then I stated my intention out loud.

"Here my friend . . . this is my gift to you. You have fulfilled your obligations to me, and to everyone else. Receive my love in abundance, and use it now to break free and rise into the Light. I love you very much, and I always will. God Speed my friend."

No lightning bolts, real or imagined, came down from Heaven. I did not hear God's voice, or even Charlton Hesston's. No music of the angels, Celine Dion, or anyone else filled the sky with crescendo. Nothing!

I sat there waiting, not knowing what to do next. Within a moment, I felt Mr. Zee's presence dissolve. He didn't say goodbye, but based upon his personality, I could imagine him announcing his departure with flair:

> "Ladies and Gentlemen, 'The Zee-man' has left the building."

Fall 2010 – Hi, buddy. I love you too.

I had gained great comfort from Mr. Zee's visits. He was wherever it is that we go when we leave this world. Before he left, I was able to give him the gift of loving energy to help him on his way. Giving that final gift dissolved almost all of the guilt I had felt because of what happened, or not happened, while he was alive. I felt complete. He was in Heaven and had no need to return.

Mr. Zee returned several time in the following weeks, but only for a few seconds at a time. They were so brief that I was not sure at the time if it was him or memories in my mind playing tricks with me. Other than a momentary smile and a quick *"Hi buddy. I love you too,"* I paid them little attention. I remember telling my girlfriend at that time that Mr. Zee had come back for a few short visits but I can't remember how many or what they were about.

To be truthful I wasn't paying much attention and did not want to give it too much energy. I quietly worried that giving attention to it might somehow 'draw' Zee back into this world, and what would be the point of that.

In regards to his visits, I never told anyone except my girlfriend and one very close friend who I knew would not call the funny farm to send over a wagon to pick me up.

Now, because of his many visits since, I know he was hanging around. I just wasn't paying attention.

Fall 2012 - Too Busy Living to Notice What is Real

I got heavily involved in every day life and a year later in January 2011 I moved to Florida to bring together a business deal. The deal went south, (pardon the pun) almost as soon as I got there, so I made my way to Phoenix to visit a long time friend. I thought of Mr. Zee often but didn't notice him around. He had lived, died and gone to Heaven or Toledo or somewhere else. It was his choice and I was satisfied with that.

In the fall of 2011, I had an accident. I fell four feet off a step and landed directly on my shoulder joint. The next six weeks of physiotherapy was the most physically painful of my life.

As Vancouver was heading into winter, I decided to go south for a while to put some sun on the damage to help it heal. I returned in the spring and moved back in with my girlfriend in July. We moved in November to a house on Larson Road in North Vancouver. The house was in good shape but had been bought by a developer and was going to be torn down in a few months.

This story is far from over. Mr. Zee would return the following month and begin returning on a regular basis. The things that have happened are nothing short of extraordinary. I have experienced and seen things I never believed for a moment were possible. We will learn what happened in this visits but first there is one very important question to ask?

Why is this happening?

There are answers to that question but in order to understand them you will need to know more about the people and animals involved. Context is everything. Briefly let us return to how this all got started.

Part III - Being Blessed With Zulu and Mr. Zee

Fall 1998 - A Princess Arrives

"In the beginning, God created man, but seeing him so feeble, He gave him the cat."
~ Warren Eckstein

My partner, Tanis and I decided not to have children. We would get a cat to love instead.

We found an ad in North Vancouver's *"North Shore News."* For over twenty years, Doris Orr and a group of volunteers had been doing animal rescue on the north shore. Tanis saw Zulu's picture in Doris's weekly ad and it was love at first sight.

We called Doris. She told us that Zulu was a darling, but she warned us that she had been mistreated and needed an especially loving home.

Upon her arrival, it was evident that Zulu was not in very good shape at all. Her skin is where her fear had come to the surface and required the most attention. She had areas where there was no fur and what looked like a type of Eczema on her little body.

Our vet told us that she would need a cortisone shot every four months or so. It was the only thing that would keep her skin from eating her alive. (He also cautioned us that he didn't think the rest of her body could tolerate the amount of cortisone that she needed.)

Tanis, being the beautiful soul she is, wasn't prepared to allow Miss Zulu to die with the damage humans had caused her. She knew precisely what Zulu really needed and never hesitated.

> *I don't believe in the concept of hell, but if I did, I would think of it as filled with people who were cruel to animals.*
> ~ Gary Larson

The Healing Power of Abundance

For the next several months, every hour of every day, Zulu had no less than *three different kinds of premium quality cat food* in her food bowl at any one time. The minute its color turned the least bit off, Tanis replaced it with a fresh batch. A bowl of crunchy food was next to the soft food, for her liking, and Tanis rinsed and refreshed her water bowl several times a day. Special kitty treats were a daily offering.

Tanis talked to Zulu in a soft loving voice throughout the day, telling her that she was precious and much loved. Miss Zulu was petted and cuddled whenever she wanted, but was never forced to accept attention when she wanted to be by herself.

Zulu gradually learned that there would be no end to food, water, or anything else she needed. She was safe, dry, warm, wanted, needed, respected and most of all, deeply loved.

How Tanis handled this relationship was one of the most profound lessons of my life. I grew up experiencing love as something 'conditional' and limited. According to my parents, and almost everyone else in my world at the time, everything, including love, was a scarce resource. You had to work hard as hell for anything you got, and you could never relax, or you would starve to death.

I still struggle with those outdated ideas and beliefs to this today. Watching Tanis love Miss Zulu back to happiness and contentment was something that touched my heart at the deepest level and changed my view of the world forever.

Both Tanis and I were enriched by the gift of Miss Zulu. Tanis treated her like the Princess she was, and the Royal treatment continued for the rest of her life.

Within months, all of Miss Zulu's health issues cleared up. Gradually she settled back into being the loving and trusting animal she must have been before encountering human beings at their worst. Her gentle presence provided a softness we both cherished.

Two Cats Are Better Than One, Aren't They?

"I think we should get Miss Zulu a friend to play with."

"You want another cat?"

"Yes."

"Really?"

"Yes, Miss Zulu might get lonely all by herself."

"She looks content to me. Aren't you really saying that YOU want another cat to pamper back to life now that Zulu's healthy?"

"Well, yes, that might be one of the reasons," Tanis said with a poorly disguised twinkle in her eye. With that, we jumped in our Jimmy and were soon "rollin' down the road" in search of another "living bedroom slipper" to trip over in the middle of the night.

I was pretending to be reluctant, but in reality, I love animals more than I love most people. Of course, there had only been one vote anyway! With Tanis and Zulu on the same side, why had I invested even one 'life unit' trying to head the idea off at the pass?

Neither Tanis nor I had any concrete idea of what we were looking for. We would know it when we saw it!

We stopped at a PetSmart store to get directions to the closest SPCA. We did not know that PetSmart provided the SPCA with space in the store for a few cages where SPCA volunteers presented pets looking for a home. We started shuffling down the row behind some folks who were also looking for a new pet. Tanis was ahead of me. Suddenly she stopped.

"There he is!" she proclaimed with glee.

I peeked around her to see a big long-haired cat. He was not up at the front of the cage seeking a bit of affection or trying to get himself picked as soon as possible. Nether was he at the back of the cage, keeping himself away from people or disengaged from the process. No, this rather large fellow was sitting in the middle of the cage, casually watching the procession of people going by. He seemed to be actually smiling, but the smile was more of a smirk. I took his expressions to mean, *"Yes, I want a nice home, but I'm in no hurry. I'll know it when I see it!"*

"He's a King." Tanis advised me.

Yes, I had to admit. He looked almost regal. He was certainly handsome, and, whoopee . . . he was white, to match Zulu. Moreover, thank God, he wouldn't clash with the white furniture.

"His Kingness made no sudden move towards us. He was patient, willing to sell the idea that he didn't have a worry in the world.

"This is 'Mr. T.' the volunteer said. "His family moved away and couldn't take him with them."

I thought to myself, "Sure, that's what they always tell you, when the real reason is they couldn't get him to stop peeing in the middle of their new couch."

Ever the woman of style and coordination, Tanis chimes in, "That's great! We can continue on with the "Z" theme, as in "Zulu." We can call him 'Mr. Z' so he' feels right at home, and... they both are white to match the new couch."

I was tempted to ask, "So how come I'm not allowed to sit on this fancy new couch, but Miss Zulu and, apparently, this new character, "Mr. Z" can lie there all day, leaving behind enough hair to knit a sweater?' Quickly I opted not to ask realizing that it was better if I didn't get an answer.

Still hanging on by a thread to the idea of not adding another layer of complication to our already hectic lives, I said, "OK. He looks like the right guy. But let's sleep on it. If he's still here in the morning we'll bring him home."

Tanis's only weakness was people pleasing. She had always done more than could ever have been expected to please me. The 'pleaser' part of her reluctantly agreed, and we headed out the door for home. I had had enough of cat shopping for one day.

People, who know me well, will tell you that I somewhat narcissistic but am also very sensitive to the feelings of others. It is both a gift and a curse. As we headed down the street, I could sense something was not right. I took a quick glance over to see if something was going on with Tanis. There was. She was silent and trying to smile, and not feel or reveal that she was broken hearted.

I thought about it for a minute. Why was I hedging on something that I knew I enjoyed? There was no good reason so I looked deeper. With no 'good reason, there must be a bad reason. It only took me a minute of traipsing through my mind to realize that I was jealous. When Miss Zulu came along, I moved from number one to number two on the list of who was the most loved in the family. Adding this guy would likely bump me to number three.

I gave my head a shake. What was I thinking? Being number three wouldn't be so bad. I was already much blessed with Tanis and Miss Zulu. Adding another blessing would only make life better, no matter where I stood in the pecking order. Being with Tanis I knew there would be more than enough love to go around.

I also realized that I was already missing 'His Royal Zeeness.' I slowed down, made an illegal U-turn in the middle of the street, and put my food down on the accelerator, headed quickly back from where we came.

"What are you doing?" Tanis asked, momentarily not remembering that I actually had a heart and every once in a while, I let it lead my decisions and actions.

"I am going back to get the King" I said as I picked up speed.

Driving faster than normal, I couldn't a take chance to look over at Tanis, but I could sense her happiness had suddenly filled the cab of our truck. I recognized the feeling as being like it had when we had first met. Our relationship had never been easy, but our love of pets was something we both shared. It provided much togetherness for us that we often had trouble generating on our own.

As a trained relationship counselor (somewhat ironic if you know my relationship history) it is said: *"When your woman is happy, you are happy."* I immediately sensed I was happier because I was showing her that I loved her by honoring her and her feminine intuition.

I thought to myself, "Such a large benefit for such a small act... how many years is it going to take for me to learn to respond this way most of the time?"

We hurried into the store, both smiling from ear to ear, and went straight to Mr. T's cage.

Empty! He was gone!

I felt my heart sink, and Tanis's sink even lower. Immediately I thought to myself, "Once again, Boy Wonder, you've screwed up."

How could that be? We had been gone less than twenty minutes.

With poorly concealed disappointment, I asked, *"Did someone already take our new, um, the white cat home?"*

The volunteer tried not to show her understanding grin too much. She explained that they rotate the cats throughout the day so they don't get stressed from all the people.

"He has been taken back to the Cat Lady's house," she told us.

"The CAT Lady?" I asked.

"Yes. The Cat Lady as she is known, lives down near the Pattullo bridge. She operates a shelter and always has about sixty cats in her house at any one time."

I thought to myself, "Sixty cats in one house. and several of them abused. God, there must be fur and cat poop flying all over the place!"

"Can we go there now?" I asked. "What's the address?"

Tanis had made her way over to the cages, just in case we were going to have to choose again.

"Don't worry, honey. We'll find him."

"Let's go," I said, and we headed quickly for the door.

For some reason, I found myself a little frantic to get there as soon as possible. I was worried that "Mr. T" would be scared out of his wits or even worse, getting beat up.

They had told us that the 'Cat Lady's' house was "under the bridge" and "across the tracks," but what a pleasant surprise it was. It was clean, smelled fine, and was, as advertised, full of cats. The lady was a real dear. She toured us through several rooms, all of them full of cats that appeared to be feeling settled and safe. She seemed to know each one of them by name.

"Some will never leave here.," she told us. "They have been too badly mistreated. But many of them will find homes when they're ready."

"How long does that take?" I asked.

"As long as it takes," she answered. "We never put a cat down here, unless it is too sick."

We entered another room full paws, tails and whiskers where we located our guy. There he was, in all his grandeur sitting high on a perch, overlooking his subjects, Quiet and confident, his stance said that he was in control. But I spotted the facade. The look behind his calm demeanor told me he was pretty scared!

'Mr. T,' we have come to take you home." Tanis said quietly, not wanting to disappoint the other cats.

She picked him up in her arms. I could see that 'Mr. T' was already falling into the 'love trap' that Tanis sets for everyone who crosses her path.

After making a donation, we put him in our kitty cage and left for home. We both agreed that Miss Zulu was going to be so pleased with us for bringing her a new friend.

> "I love cats because I enjoy my home; and little by little they become it's visible soul."
> ~ **Jean Cocteau**

The Walking Hair Ball

Tanis sat down on her knees in front of our kitty cage. I opened the door as she offered her two open hands. Without a second of hesitation, 'Mr. T' walked out of the cage and into Tanis's loving arms. She held him up to her face so he could see her smile.

"Welcome to your new home Mr. ZEE."

Knowing first hand that a 'Tanis hug' could melt the heart of even the wildest of beasts, (me) I knew we were off to a good start.

Putting him down softly Mr. Zee promptly hopped onto Tanis's new white couch. By the smile on his whiskery face, I could see he was working this for all it was worth. Circling around to find the whitest spot Zee flopped down and then looked at us as if to say,' "This will do quite nicely. I will be King and you my subjects. What has the cook prepared for dinner?"

"All is well in the Kingdom, "I thought, "but the moment of truth will soon be upon us."

Our little princess came around the corner of the couch, took one look at 'Mr. Zee,' decided he was a monster, of some unknown origin, and almost jumped out of her skin, literally! I mean, she was so shocked she instantly expelled much of her entire coat of hair. Then, she took off at lightning speed, leaving behind a big pile of hair, with a hole in the middle, where a cat had been just a second ago.

"Not exactly the 'love at first sight' we had hoped for," I casually tossed into the silence.

Tanis winked at me and giggled. She would make everything perfect, as she always did.

But Zulu never relented. She never made friends with Zee. He attempted all kinds of 'cat type' gestures of affection, but Zulu wouldn't entertain any of it. He kept trying to be pals for a week or two, but t princess would just hiss and keep backing up into the closest corner she could find.

Over the years, they came to be friends 'from afar,' never really cuddling, but often sitting side-by-side, each pretending not to be aware of the other. Zulu did finally let Zee come close and lick her coat, but that was only when she was very sick, and a few days from her passing.

Saving Our Princess

For some unknown reason white cats are prone to losing the use of their hind legs.

Zulu began to stumble as she jumped off the couch; at the time we thought it was funny and we would giggle, believing it was harmless. But she then progressed to hardly being able to walk across a room without toppling over and finally to crawling along dragging her hindquarters behind her.

I took her for ultrasound, (which cost over a thousand dollars), but they saw nothing that indicated why this was happening, and offered no solution. Miss Zulu was going to leave us, and no amount of love was going to save her this time.

The pain was too much for Tanis to bear. She did not want to take the chance of Zulu suffering, and wanted to put her down right away.

I hesitated. Zulu didn't seem to be in any pain. If she could still get to her food bowl and had an appetite, she was functioning as she would have if she were in nature, even though we were making her daily 'prey' readily available, without her having to hunt it down.

"When she is no longer able to get to her food bowl, it will be time," I said. "Before that time, she is our responsibility and in our hands. After that she will be in God's."

At the time, I was not much of a believer in God, but Tanis was. My words consoled her for the time being, so she agreed to wait.

We went on for about a month, and I don't regret it for a minute. Zulu did not seem to be in pain. She seemed a bit lost as to the reason this was happening to her, but I could feel her acceptance. She knew her time was near, and gave no indication of any need to fight the process.

I have come to believe that some things we go through in life are actually lessons we need to learn. But, they are lessons we can learn them in no other way, except by going through what we are going through at the time. The more fully we embrace what is happening, the richer the lesson and the farther it takes us forward in our spiritual development.

> (One of my teachers, Dr. Chuck Spezzano, who has had over 100,000 people attend his seminars on Higher Vision says that choosing to embrace rather than avoid even one of these lessons can save us a thousand years.)

Yes, our hearts were breaking as we stepped around what we knew was the inevitable, but I felt that all three of us were there for a reason. I didn't know what those reasons were for me, and certainly not for Tanis or Miss Zulu, but I sensed it was something about learning to feel the full range of emotions, no matter whether they are ecstatic joy or they hurt like hell.

At that time I was working mostly at home, so I was available to tend to Miss Zulu's needs. Each day I lifted her up onto my desk beside me, or placed her onto my lap. She slept most of the time, and when she was not sleeping, she was purring. She would look up at me with her beautiful eyes and just blink, which is a cat's way of saying, "I see you and yes I think you are wonderful too."

I spent the time we had together not trying to change anything, but rather just loving her. I didn't say much. Instead, I let my heart just feel and expand the love I had for her, and let as much of it as I could envelop her. Zulu returned my love with more of the same sometimes almost more than I could receive without becoming overwhelmed. I will never forget how we just soaked up each other's love.

The day came when she messed all over her thick white coat, and I had to wash her in the sink for almost an hour to get her white and clean again. That was the decision point for me. I was not about to allow my need to have her with me cause our proud Miss Zulu the lose of her dignity. The time Tanis and I were silently dreading so much had come.

At Home In Our Arms

We asked our Vet, Steve, who had treated Miss Zulu for the last few years, to come over to the house. I was so glad we did. When I opened the front door to let Steve in, the look on his face was equal to the sadness that must have been on our own.

Steve quickly set a calm, quiet and respectful tone, which really helped Tanis and I settle our nerves. Steve explained that he would give Miss Zulu two injections. The first one was meant only to relax her, and dissolve away any stress, fear or pain. The second would stop her heart. It would take affect in only take a second or two and she would be gone.

Tanis could not bear it. Hearing this, she took off out of the room. I followed a couple of minutes later with a strong sense of what to say. I found our bedroom door closed with Tanis sobbing deeply inside. I waited for a minute or so to honor her breaking heart.

Speaking quietly I said I felt she should come back and be close to Zulu.

"Honey I think it's important that she feels our love around her when she goes. To not be with her would be a loss to all of us. We need to cherish her and honor all the love she had brought us and send her off with our deepest blessings.

Tanis, tears falling down her beautiful Scottish cheeks, took my hand. She knew that what I was saying was right. Hand in hand, we rejoined Steve and Zulu in the family room.

Steve nodded respectfully to both of us and gently gave our little princess the first injection. Almost instantly, I knew we had made the right choice to move forward on this day.

The moment the first drug took effect Zulu's whole demeanor changed almost instantly. The pain that we had not noticed before, evaporated. She relaxed and gave a sweet sigh of relief. Then she did something that surprised me. She regained enough of her muscle control to a take long glorious stretch, the kind that cats do after they wake up from a really refreshing nap. She had not been able to move like that for months. Zulu seemed relieved and comfortable again. She was happy, like I remembered her before she got sick.

Steve nodded to me. I drew her up in my arms. Zulu was at home and she was with people she knew loved her with all their hearts. I met her eyes. I cannot imagine feeling more love ever again. Tanis stroked her head as Steve applied the second drug. She gave one short kick, as if to scratch her belly, and then she was free forever.

We held her for a long minute more, to assist her transition, as her life force released from her body. Then we gently placed her in a little casket that Tanis had lovingly constructed out of a pretty jewel box she cherished.

A few minutes later, as I was about to take her out to the grave I had dug in the back yard, Mr. Zee came round the corner. He walked over to where Zulu was laying and took a long sniff, then paused for about ten seconds, which is probably cat's equivalent to a moment of silence. Our big fella then turned slowly around and made his way out of the room. He withdrew to the safety of his favorite hiding spot and would not make his way back to his old self for a few days. It took me a few weeks to grieve the loss. Tanis continues to hold her precious princess in her heart to this day.

How do our pets nestle so deeply into our hearts? I do not know but it is their gift to us. They show us a depth of love within us that we could not likely have reached on our own.

Part IV – The King and I

Summer 2005 - Two Bachelors in Marpole

Several months after Miss Zulu passed Tanis and I decided to go our separate ways. Tanis got the car and I got the cat. I moved from White Rock into Vancouver and settled into a two-bedroom apartment in Marpole.

Mr. Zee and I considered ourselves two bachelors sharing the same space. As I worked mostly at home, we spent a lot of time together.

We had a very simple agreement. I was to give him my undivided attention whenever he asked for it. I was to leave him to hell alone when he didn't. I was to feed him throughout the day, at any time of his choosing. I was to be home first thing in the morning to feed him no matter what else I had going on. The food was to be fresh and of good quality. If none of the above were acceptable to me I could go live somewhere else but the furniture was all his if I did.

His part of the agreement, according to him, was to make my life both a frustration and a 'rolling on the floor' joy at the same time.

Mr. Zee was a cat of fine but no particular breeding... he had long hair... lots of hair... and it was white... long, white that shed in never ending abundance. He cost me at least two (sneezing, wheezing, dress covered in white hair, girlfriends). I like to wear black. He was always with me where ever I went.

> *"All of the animals, except for man, know that the principle business of life is to enjoy it."*
> ~ Samuel Butler

Swish Go the Glasses

Zee was smarter than your average cat, and he was totally committed to packing as many grins and giggles into life as possible, regardless of the consequences.

Mr. Zee was an early riser. After all, if you are going to fill your life with 'hell raising' you have to be committed to a certain work ethic, including the idea that if getting started early was good, then getting up earlier was even better.

Every bloody morning, 'General Zee' would awaken at around 4:00 AM (sometimes earlier) and want to be fed, "Right now!"

Mr. Zee was not someone who took a groggy "No," for an answer. Nor was he someone who would take "NO! NO! NO!" for an answer, either. "Bugger off, you goddamn cat!" had no noticeable effect, except to be the clue that he would have to employ some much more intense tactics in order to ensure that the mission would be successful.

The following can best be described as a cat's version of psychological warfare. Now, stay with me, here. There are multiple steps in the 'Battle of Marpole Chow.' The strategy and tactics employed by our 'white warrior of entitlement' would have made Generals Montgomery, Eisenhower and Patton all bow in total respect.

Step 1: 4:00 AM - Jump onto the bed and begin a heavy-footed walk around the still body lying therein. Repeat, if necessary.

Step 2: 4:01 AM - If unsuccessful, jump on body, sometimes referred to as 'Master,' and then run away quickly to the food dish in the kitchen. Repeat, as necessary.

Step 3: If step 2 does not produce a fresh breakfast after a couple of tries, jump up onto the dresser located next to bed, and look for loose change. If successful, act like you'd never seen coins before and pounce on it, then swish it off the dresser onto the floor with paw.

Step 4: Turn around and face Master, so as not to get caught using paw. Use tail to swish off remaining change. Look at Master as if you are having so much fun you could easily keep this up for hours.

Step 5: Stop swishing tail when Master looks up. Look away as if nothing has happened and assume innocent expression. If accused, 'plead the fifth,' claiming the tail has a mind of it's own and is not under your direct control, especially when you are hungry, or when you are mad. Claim you lose control completely of that unruly tail when you are both hungry *and* mad.

Step 6: If no attempt is made by Master's body to get out of bed, find reading glasses on the dresser. Swish said glasses off the dresser onto floor. Aim for freshly swished change that is already on the floor, as it always produces a louder sound, the sound that indicates the need of repairs at the nice Optometrist's office down the street. Listen for louder 'comments. A disgruntled voice confirms that the glasses are a 'high value target' and thus likely to produce the intended results.

Step 7: Leave the battlefield on the run, and head for said food bowl. Try not to appear too happy as heavy-footed slippers drag themselves across the floor to where the provisions are stored.

Step 8: Begin to circle the food bowl, rapping tail around Master's leg as fresh rations are being spooned in. Begin eating immediately,  so as to not appear to be celebrating the victory over 'the stupid one' again. Make notes of any revisions needed to be made to the old, but highly effective 'Feed Me or Face The Consequences' Maneuver.'

Step 9: Eat the 'Salmon Benny' as if it is being served at the Waldorf Astoria, and head back to bed to prepare for another long stretch of intensive napping.

Step 10 - Plop down onto whatever part of 'the stupid one' is the warmest. So as to avoid suspicion, change this up a bit by lying down just above stupid one's' head on the pillow. Enjoy several minutes of intense fur licking. Get up, re-evaluate location. Test new choice by twisting and turning to make sure the spot is completely satisfactory.

Step 11 - Assume cute, loving look to solicit petting. Begin purring loudly so 'the stupid one' will forgive and forget that the main goal is to intimidate his butt out of bed and get him to work early, so that the Salmon Benny's will continue uninterrupted for many years to come.

Step 12: Enjoy pre-warmed bed, and now vacated bed. Fall asleep. Remain asleep for as long as possible. Plan tomorrow's 'special opps' upon awakening.

By this final step, I would be very much awake and needing a cup of coffee to settle my nerves down from the fog of war.

This battle went on for several years. As much fun as it is to write about now, I sometimes wonder if a slight bit of the PTSD I have is a result of encountering Mr. Zee's persistence.

Mr. Zee had too many games to mention, but there was one incident I remember that draws a big smile out of me whenever I think of it.

"A Moose Loose In The Hoose"

3:00 AM! I awake to hear, "Thump, thump, thump' coming from the living room. "Thump*, thump, thump . . . thump, thump THUMP."* I let it go on for a minute or two longer, but it is starting to drive me nuts, (which, Mr. Zee would say, is a short trip.)

"*What the hell is going on?*" I ask myself out loud. "Is my roommate having a party or something?"

I do the 'dead man slipper shuffle' into the living room. Flicking the light switch, I see Mr. Zee has a mouse that, through my not yet focused eyes, seems to be alive, but is already beginning to look like a stale hors d'oeuvre.

'Zee Man,' being the kind soul that I convinced everybody he was, had caught a mouse. Just for the fun of it, he was allowing it to run frantically back and forth across the room, attempting to escape. Zee would wait a couple of seconds, then run to the end of the room where the mouse appeared to have almost made his escape. Then he would chase it back to the other end of the living room to cut off the mouse's next attempt at freedom.

Loads of fun for Mr. Zee. For the mouse?... Not so much.

The poor critter was, with good reason, afraid for his life and looked like he was pretty sure he wasn't going to like the end of this story.

I said..."Mr. Zee, what the hell are you doing? It's three o'clock in the morning! Cut out the thump, thump, thumping already" and with that I picked up the mouse and tossed it, out the kitchen window, onto the grass.

Mr. Zee looked in my direction, promptly offering his, "Aw come on. When did you lose your sense of humour?" Then he turned his head and stared in any direction except mine. His face revealed that he was not impressed with my obvious ignorance to a few million years of cat DNA. But, hey, he was living rent free, so he knew he didn't really have a paw to stand on.

Having saved the mouse from his almost certain demise, I turned off the lights and shuffled back from whence I came, to a now ice cold bed, best explained as Vancouver's version of sleeping in a tent in Antarctica.

The light bulb in my bedroom hadn't even lost its glow when again I heard, *"Thump, thump, thump."* The sound was noticeably quieter this time, probably so it wouldn't invoke "the grumpy bugger" (that would be me) to start yelling again. His strategy did not work. I hollered, *"Don't you make me come out there again or no Salmon Bennies for a week!"*

Zee, knowing he must get in as much practice as he could for the 'annual mouse hunt in the fall,' considered my threat, and rejected it out of hand. This was all 'just too damn much fun.'

Our 'great white hunter' jumped outside through the window I had so considerately left open for him, and re-acquired the mouse, which, no doubt, had been running for his bloody life!

Zee had returned the mouse to his indoor running track and was thoroughly enjoying Round Two of, *"There's A Moose Loose in the Hoose."*

I decided to leave the mouse to find his 'gladiator within.' and rolled over. I simply had to accept that I was a mere servant to this incredible being, who had a strong sense of pride, entitlement and confidence in who he was: "The King of All Things Cat."

Many times, as I observed him, I was convinced he must had been the King of Camelot in a past life, and he had been obeyed and well respected.

Living In Close

"Lots of people talk to animals. Not very many listen though. That's the problem."
~ Benjamin Hoff

I live in Vancouver. It rains in Vancouver. From November to February you might as well build an Ark and just wait for the water to lift it off its moorings. Being from the prairies where the sun shines all winter I don't do 'soggy' well at all.

For those four months, when I'm not travelling, I don't go out. I hole up in my apartment and write books and articles, watch TV, ponder the deeper aspects of life, eat, and sleep. During this time, Mr. Zee and I spent long periods of time together.

At times like these, when a person is in seclusion, one of the things that happens is that your mind settles down and stops a lot of its useless chatter. As a result, your ability to sense subtle things, both internal and external is heightened.

In lieu of going out, and being involved in a wide social circle, I would talk to my pal Zee. As many cat lovers know, if you can get past the 'dumb animal' idea, and pay attention, you will find eventually that the pets talks back.

Mr. Zee never had a lot to say, but when he did, it was considered and direct. He would have made a good psychologist but a lousy politician.

These long periods of time spent together continued for several years. I watched this guy a lot. He was such a character. I never wanted to miss even one of his 'crimes against the mundane.'

Eventually I found that I pretty much knew what he was thinking by just looking at the expression on his face. Sometimes he was in deep thought; sometimes he had a smirk on his face. He had no hesitation showing me he was not particularly impressed with some of the ways I approached life, especially when I came home late for dinner.

"Where The Hell Have You Been?"

If I was delayed or away over night, and I didn't rush home to feed his Zeeness, he would be waiting for me at the door. "*Meow, meow, meow.*" (Translation: "Where the hell have you been? You are late again!") "'*Meow Meow, meow*"' ("You know how I hate to wait for my breakfast and be late for my morning nap.") '*Meow, Meow, MEOW.*' (You know Hunkin; you are a real asshole sometimes. I don't know why I put up with you. Come on... get your act together fella or I'm going to start waking you up at '*2:30'*in the morning).

It would take him up to a day after each one of these late returns for him to give me the time of day. The cat had balls well, not really, but you get what I mean.

Our Daily Snooze

Sometime around the seventh year of our relationship, I took to having a nap each day at around 4:00 pm in the afternoon. Mr. Zee soon warmed to the idea as well, and began to join me for a daily siestas. He loved to be refreshed for the evening meal and a good night of television.

It never ceased to amaze me how, no matter how deeply a sleep he was in, or what remote part of the apartment he was located, he always knew the precise second I laid down for a nap. Consistently, within no more than two minutes, he hopped on to my bed and began preparing to join me in a rejuvenating slumber.

I got to know every movement and sensation of his jumping on my bed, walking around my legs until he found just the right spot to wash himself, and then flopping down, leaning against my leg or arm. Often I sleep with my legs open. He would walk up and snuggle down between my knees to take advantage of the warmth and protection available there.

(I was to learn later that there was a real benefit in knowing how each one of his movements felt)

The Scratching Ritual

A few months after we started having a daily nap together, I started a scratching and rubbing routine that I deliberately conducted in the same way every day.

Before we nodded off, I would start by putting my one hand on his shoulder and giving him a bit of a hug. (Thanks for coming, I love you,) then three or four scratches under his chin with my fingers,(Let's go for the mother lode right away, Zee man) then scratching on the left cheek, then the right cheek (he loved the left one more, so we always took the time for an extra scratch or two there. (Here buddy, I know you can't scratch these yourself), then three or four scratches behind the right ear, then behind the left, then under his chin and in his mane under his neck, first on one side, then the other.

I would work my way down his spine, massaging with both hands from his neck to his bum, which always lifted up when I reached it. ("Still got some of the old tomcat zip there, don't you good buddy?") He seemed to have a memory of his testosterone from a times long ago, but he never could quite remember what and how it went missing.) Finally, a couple of scratches on his shanks to finish off.

In our daily "Scratch and Love" ritual, he would never let me rub his eyes or eyebrows. It took him over two years to trust me enough to even allow me to lightly stroke both of his eyes and eyebrows with the back of my finger. (For those of you that want to try this technique, I suggest you always stroke from the nose outward.) After being reluctant to allow me to touch his eyes like this for so long, he came to realize that he really enjoyed this part of the process. Later on, it became his very favourite part of our daily massage date and he would push his face right into my hand. We had started working on his paws that were equally as guarded, but didn't get all the way there before he was killed.

When we finished the routine Mr. Zee would relax down onto my chest for our snooze together He fell asleep right away while I, on the other hand, had to concentrate on letting go of the many thoughts bouncing around in my head. Both of us were sleeping within about five minutes.

Thirty to forty-five minutes later, I would awaken to see Zee still flopped out across my chest, dead to the world. I suppose he knew that he was safe and could just let go completely.

Sometimes I would open my eyes to see him looking at me… actually, it seemed like he was looking 'into' me.

The Zen of Scratch

I have done quite a bit of 'personal research' on the impact that shame, guilt and regret has on our lives. To summarize, these emotions and beliefs cause us to hide from others and ourselves. We keep ourselves separate physically, mentally, emotionally and spiritually from everyone (including ourselves). The ability to reveal ourselves to ourselves increasingly seeing our own innocence and value, is an aspect of what I call 'Worthiness.'

> (I have been researching Worthiness since 1994 and I documented what I learned in a book called 'Your Worthiness Cycle.' Published by Amazon May 2013)

In my own personal growth process, I decided to learn how to and practice letting my true self see and be seen. I added a connection exercise to 'The Daily Scratch' routine with Zee.

Sometimes, when I woke up, I would find Mr. Zee already awake and looking at me... directly at me. (rare for a cat) I would focus and look as deeply as I could into his eyes as well.

The objective of the exercise was to continue to look into the eyes of 'Other' (What Martin Buber refers to as "Thou") and allow myself be seen for as long as I could tolerate such an intimate connection without looking away.

(This exercise is the foundation for all authentically intimate communication. It is what Landmark Education calls "being with.")

It is true definition of Intimacy... **'Into YOU See Me'**

Looking away, or separating oneself from that connection with another is caused by a thought that makes us feel anxious and believe we are not worthy to receive the overwhelming amount of love we are experiencing in that moment of complete presence.

Mr. Zee was a lot better at this loving gaze than I was. He would look deeply into me with his big blue eyes and not turn away. I had to really concentrate on staying aware and present, and being able to recognize when a thought was coming that would invoke the response of turning away.

Catching this disruptive thought early in the process of connecting is the key. With practice, you can get to the point where you can watch each thought form on the horizon of your mind, observe it coming to you, entering you, passing through you, and then finally traveling away from you.

Psychologically, there is no pain in the present moment. If you are in pain then some part of your mind stuck in the past.

Learning to be 'the observer' allows you to choose what value you attach to any one though. The more you are 'in the present moment' the more likely you are to let the thought drifty by rather than letting it cause a reaction based on the past i.e. fear, worry, regret etc.

At first, I could not continue my love broadcast for more than a few seconds. I could not resist the need to turn my eyes away. Within a month or two, I got up to about 30 seconds.

My friend Michael Ledwith *('What The Bleep Do We Know')* says that a group he was involved with did a similar exercise using a candle. It took experienced practitioners, doing daily practice, two years or more, to be able to continue the Love Gaze for at least 90 seconds. It seems we humans 'think' we have many reasons to not receive Love in abundance.

Whenever I was clear enough of my own fears, shame and judgments, towards myself and others, I would see what I came to know as my highest self, being reflected back from Zee's loving gaze. For man it is a rare experience indeed, but perhaps a lot more frequent for Beast.

> *"If a dog will not come to you after having looked you in the face you should go home and examine your conscience."*
> **~ Woodrow Wilson**

Needless to say, this created an even deeper bond between Zee and I.

The Importance of Bonding

Being an adopted child, I was swept up away from my mother at the time of my birth, never to feel her loving embrace again.

Though this was the practice of the day, since that time, the importance of establishing an attachment between a mother figure and the newborn infant has been discovered. Subsequent research has demonstrated that 'skin to skin' bonding with the mother, especially within the first hour after birth plays a huge role in successful transition into this sometimes frightening world.

The research demonstrates that the sense of confidence and security engendered by this bonding experience endures throughout a lifetime. Because of this research, today, even a child that is being put up for adoption is returned to its mother's chest immediately after birth to ensure that the attachment is established. Apparently the fulfillment of this simple instinctual need for skin contact assures the newborn infant that the connection they had with their mother in the womb is real and has not been lost now that they are out in the world and on their own. The importance of this connection cannot be overstated.

Not having the benefit of a mother's love at birth physically, I had decided that the feeling of being bonded was just an illusion. To be truthful, I did not really believe *'Unconditional'* Love existed either. Eventually I figured out that Connection and Love was real, but in an inverse way, *by the extreme lack of it.*

I never believed in any of it until my son was born. My son is the only person with whom I have a direct blood (energetic) connection. I experience a completely different group of feelings, when my son gives me a hug, than I do with any other person on the planet.

Up until that first hug, I could *'talk'* about bonding but had not yet experienced truce Connection in my body. I'm sure that you can imagine how internally conflicted I was as a professional speaker speaking about personal growth. I felt like an imposter a lot of the time because I was telling folks things that I did not really believe, only suspected.

Because of my experiences with my son, Mr. Zee and others I have come to believe that a deep profound love and connection is possible between all beings. Any Connection lost can be regained.

Mr. Zee's visits have finally allowed me to accept that Connection, Bonding and Love transcends our local experience of our mind and body. As you read, Mr. Zee provided that proof to me in very direct, personal and profound ways.

> *"If having a soul means being able to feel love and loyalty and gratitude, then animals are better off than a lot of humans."*
> **~ James Herriot**

For the next six years, Mr. Zee and I lived these rituals and experiences repeatedly.

Gateways to the Paranormal

This section of the book has provided some of the factors I believe were responsible for me experiencing Mr. Zee returning from the afterlife. The closeness, bonding and connection that we established all played a role in allowing these incredible paranormal experiences to happen.

In Part I through Part III you learned about this incredible being named Mr. Zee. You have gotten to know how he was (is) a real character, full of fun and frolic. You learned how he died and about the incredible experience of his return from beyond the veil and that he had returned a few more times between 2010 and 2012.

In the next Part, you will read how the frequency of his visits along with their duration increased to the point where he would be/is with me for several nights in a row. You are going to be introduced to other cats that began coming along with him.

All of this is based upon based upon notes taken by me 'in real time.'

We now move forward in time to the fall of 2012 and early 2013.

SpiritArt

A Painting by *Catresea Ann Canivan*

Part V - The Whole Game Changes

January 2013 - Am I Going Nuts?

I climbed into bed and had barely pulled the covers up when I felt a bit of movement rustling around my feet. Mr. Zee was under the covers. He seemed to be looking for something.

Then next night he came again and the night after that. I was not asleep or in a dream. In fact, I had not even fully settled into the bed before he arrived. By the third night, I was really beginning to question my sanity.

Thank God for Google

This time he had stayed for at least 2 hours. I checked the clock. It was 2:30 in the morning. I rolled out of bed and quickly booted my computer. If this is actually happening then others must have experienced the same thing, at least I certainly hoped so.

I have done many Google searches for various projects. I find what I am looking for pretty quickly. It is true that if you know the right question to ask the answer reveals itself soon after.

The Good News - Others Are Nuts Too!

I searched 'ghost cat on bed.' Sure enough, there were a couple of dozen posts from people whose pet had died and who had experienced them returning. Some told of single visits, while others reported multiple visits spread over a period of time. As many pets sleep on the same bed as their masters, it seemed the bed was the most common location for return visits. (See Appendix for links to other stories of animals returning.)

It was at this point that I decided to start making notes. I decided to begin an intelligent, methodical and scientific approach to recording and analyzing these occurrences, rather than just consistently be amazed and frightened by what was happening, and what might happen next.

My passion is and always has been to help people live a fully empowered life full of Success, Happiness and Fulfillment. If there were lessons for me to learn here then maybe they also apply to other people. I felt that, in the matter of spirits jumping around on your bed, people deserved to read as complete and accurate a accounting as I could muster. With enough data, based upon the facts, as I knew them, people would be able to decide for themselves what was true for them and how it applies to their life.

Most people I found on the Internet, who have had a similar experience, had done a single blog/forum post about what had happened. From reading these posts it seemed that my experience was much more expansive, in number of visits, the duration of each visit and the length of time that these visitations have been going on since Zee's death.

Initially I waited until the morning after to document what had happened, but once I started to consider writing this book, I started making my notes immediately after Mr. Zee's visit.

Later I dictated into my iPhone, in real time, to document what was happening as accurately as possible. Mr. Zee had always responded well to my voice so he seemed reassured that I was present when he heard me speaking. When speaking softly into recorder some of the more subtle movements and sensations diminished slightly.

Mr. Zee returned many time throughout the month of January and has continued his visits since. He does not come every night but often for two or three nights in a row then skips a few nights, then returns again for another three or four nights.

As the visits increased in frequency, I started to notice and keep track of the commonality of the activities, movements and sensations from one visit to the next.

Many Questions

There are many questions to be answered. Answering them can have a profound impact on the way we view life, death and dying.

1. Why did Mr. Zee return the first time?
2. Why does he continue to return?

3. Why me? Is there anything unique about me that causes this to happen?
4. What did I do, if anything, to encourage or facilitate Mr. Zee coming back, not only once or twice, but dozens and dozens of times since the first encounter?
5. What did Mr. Zee do to make it possible for him to come back and forth?
6. What do we do together that made this relationship possible?
7. What am I doing before, during, and after these visits that is causing the frequency and intensity to increase?
8. Why now? Why did Mr. Zee come back now?
9. What is the purpose of these visits? Is there something he wants me to know, or, perhaps, do for him?
10. Has something changed that makes it easier for him to pass back and forth through the veil between life and the afterlife?
11. What is actually happening here, in purely scientific terms?
12. How do Zee and his fellow cats do it?
13. What are they experiencing?
14. Can other people share in my experience?
15. Can other people do specific things to enable their pets to return once or multiple times?

Throughout the remainder of the book, I will address as many of these questions as possible. Some questions will be answered to everyone's satisfaction. Some will be left for others to answer.

I hope that the answers I have received to these questions may help to provide more pet owners with the opportunity to experience their pets returning home. I believe that, if the process can be refined, it can open up a completely new portal through the veil between life here and in the next dimension.

Part V describes to the best of my ability what Mr. Zee and others cats are doing while they are with me.

For Updates, visit MrZeeComesHome.com

Part VI - Movements, Sensations and Feelings

I feel it is important that you know what is going on and what I am experiencing throughout these visits.

> This whole experience has convinced me that many pets return after death to be with those whom they love. I suspect that this happens all the time but people do not recognized the movements and sensations for what they really are. Was that tickle on the side of your leg just something that needed to be scratched or was it your beloved pets whiskers or tail swishing back and forth? If you are aware of what to look for you have a much better change of understanding these communications from some other reality/ dimension/Universe or from heaven, whatever word works for you.

In my particular experience, the visits start at the foot of the bed, usually within less than a minute of getting under the covers. I feel either a hop up from the floor at the foot of the bed, a general arrival of something taking shape, or a kind of silent 'pop' as if the cat is appearing out of nowhere.

Mr. Zee begins to walk back and forth from the left side of my left foot to the right side of my right foot. He sometimes pauses in the middle. If I open my legs as I often did when he was 'alive' he will sometimes enters the space between my legs and walks up part way before either lying down or turning around and walking back towards my feet.

Lying on My Chest

When he was alive, he spent so much time lying on my chest that I expected he would make his way there but he cannot seem to do it. I tried to encourage him by patting my chest to make the sound that I always used to invite him to come up.

A few times, it felt as if he was starting to walk up onto my chest (from either side) but he has never made it all the way. The second he tried he disappeared and then reappears down by my feet or beside my leg within a few seconds.

I have given the question some thought... Why hasn't he been able to lie on my chest or why does he dissolve when he tries to do so. I'm pretty sure Mr. Zee knows more about this than I do so perhaps he knows that it would be too intense for one or the other of us or both. Possibly, it would be harmful in some way. Maybe he knows he might actually be drawn into my chest and/or heart with unknown consequences.

Rolling Over

Most of the time, when I get into bed I first lie down on my back and then after a minute or two I roll over onto my right side. Mr. Zee also appears when I am lying on my side or stomach. I have felt him tuck in beside my upper leg as I was on my side. A few times, as I am drifting off to sleep and begin to roll over, (which would have result in me rolling on top of him), he jumps up and moves away to a safe distance. I first feel extra pressure against my leg as he pushes himself up and then he moves so I can continue to roll over without squishing him underneath.

Purring

After several visits my fear and anxiety subsided. I was able to pay more attention to each one of my senses (seeing, feeling, hearing, etc.) to observe what sense were being stimulated.

On the second or third visit, I thought that I heard a purring sound. It was very faint, like someone talking but way off in another room. As I had not actually noticed when it started, I thought maybe I was just 'hearing things.' No, the next visits proved that he was in-fact purring I heard the purring start and then when it quit (unless I fell asleep).

Like the pitch of our voice, each cat has his or her own purring signature. The differences are quite subtle but are there nevertheless. Very early, when the visits began, I had worried that maybe it was a raccoon or a boa constrictor or something else more sinister. Although faint, the purring was one of the reasons, I was quite sure it was Mr. Zee. He had purred for hours on my chest so I had experienced his purr deep within me. It was Mr. Zee all right, in all his glory.

The Press, Pull and Draw

After a few visits, I began to feel him pressing against my feet, specifically my big toe. The sensation is that of a someone's finger pressing on the middle of your big toe and attempting to push it back over center.

Over the course of a few more visits, the pressure increased and became quite strong. I worried that my toe might be bent back so far that it might break off. After a few visits the pressure evened out a bit.

The sensation morphed into one of my toe being pulled up and away from my foot. Then it transformed again into a feeling as if something were drawing on it.

The 'drawing' sensations feel as if something has put its mouth around my toe and is sucking on it. I do not feel lips or teeth biting down but more like a sucking feeling. I can often feel the tongue moving back and forth.

From Toes to Fingers and Back Again

On my invitation, Zee will make his way up to my hands, and, as he does with my feet, he presses on my thumbs, and, sometimes, on my fingers. Once, it became almost painful as he was pushing too hard. The pushing then gives way to the drawing or sucking feeling on my thumbs.

My ego mind goes crazy with fearful questions. "What if he suddenly takes a bite out of my hand? Will chunk of skin come off? Will I bleed? Will it leave a scab or a scar?"

Then my thoughts become completely irrational.

"Will my head start twisting around and around, full circle, like in the movie 'The Exorcist? I don't think so, but who knows?"

Scratching Favourite Places

After several visits to my feet, legs and fingers, I got the idea to invite Mr. Zee to come up and get a "Scratch and Love" massage, just like we used to do when he was in physical form. Our regular scratching ritual had been the highlight of his day, except, of course, the part when he was terrorizing me to get up.

I moved my right hand under the covers and scratched the bottom sheet with my fingers to make the usual 'invitation' sound with which he was so familiar. I did it two more times and then, as if noticing and remembering something, he stopped moving back and forth, changed direction, and headed up towards my right hand.

We continue to share this routine to this day. Sometimes he comes from as far away as the lower outside of my left foot. Sometimes he walks over my leg. Sometimes he kind of hops over it. Sometimes it feels like he walks 'threw' my legs. I do not feel any sensation of him passing through my skin and bones but it is as if his steps are not interrupted and I feel no extra pressure on the mattress as I would if he hopped over.

Performing "The Scratch" is a very important juncture, because it means we are both aware of my command to come, and his response of coming. This confirms that I am in direct communication with him, rather than him just appearing and then doing things at random, without my having any interaction with him.

The Chin and Belly

The first three times he came up to my right hand I had felt him press against my fingers with some part of him but I did not know which part. I then reasoned that if he were coming to my hand he would want to be scratched on his chin because that was his favorite.

I turned my right hand over so that my fingers were pointed up. I made the movement of scratching in mid air starting at my little finger and rapidly closing each finger in succession ending with my index.

Mr. Zee immediately made his way up to my right hand as I continued to beckon with my fingers.

Hair and Whiskers

After about 15 seconds, I began to feel something. It took me a minute or so to realize I was actually feeling the hair on the bottom of his chin.

I felt him pressing his chin down onto my fingers and the hair moving in response to my scratching. There was enough pressure that I felt that there was skin holding the hair although I did not feel any actual skin or bone.

I learned that I had to keep the back of my hand on the sheet. The natural tendency is to want more of the sensation because we reason in our heads that more would make it more 'real.' If I lifted my hand up off the covers to attempt more contact with his chin the whole sensation disappeared. When I dropped my hand back onto the covers, his chin hairs would return within a few seconds.

The first time I felt his chin hairs I almost jumped out of my skin. For some reason this particular movement made everything even more true for me. I knew it was his chin having felt it many times before and he was coming on command to experience it. The thought of that was both extremely exciting and frightening at the same time.

In this instance I am in three places at the same time:

1. I am trying to calm my ego mind from throwing up fearful thoughts.
2. I am trying to not give off any fear vibes that would scare Mr. Zee and cause him to disappear, maybe forever.
3. I am staying aware of all the movements and sensations so I notice if he does something different which I do not want to miss.

Staying awake, aware, conscious and in the present moment caused me to be quite tired afterwards.

I made a note to stay awake to all the ways that my mind is trying to get the better of me. If I am vigilant, I can stop it from gaining momentum and/or power over me.

I attempted to scratch his belly as well. He moved his belly towards my hand a few times but he was never particularly fond of it in real life. Often he had jumped and bit me when I got to close to parts that he was defensive about so I was not surprised when this part of the process wasn't that attractive to him.

I *'Must'* Be Able to See Something

I had attempted to see what was happening, a few times. There had been nothing no matter how real if felt.

First, he was under the covers so I would not likely have been able to see all the way to the end of the bed in the dark. I had lifted the covers a few times with no luck.

Once he had made his way onto the top of the covers, I felt that I would have a better chance of being able to see him 'in the flesh.' The sensation of him at my hand was so real that I was convinced I would be able to see something at my side.

After a few chin rubs, I sensed that he felt safe so I took a look. Nothing! I lifted my head higher so I could see better. Not only was there no sight of him but also the minute I looked the feelings and sensations of his presence reduced by more than half.

I speculate Mr. Zee is not resisting being seen. I think it is my mind telling me that, if my eyes do not see him then what is happening is just an illusion.

Our scientifically biased education system and culture instills in us the idea that we should only believe something if we can see it and prove its existence is real. The notion that we will "see it when we believe it" is considered illogical and irrational. In fact, someone who believes that kind of nonsense is making things up. They are considered by scientists to be, at best, either naïve and gullible, or, at worst, completely insane. Alternatively, sometimes this kind of inexplicable phenomenon is relegated to the realm of Spiritual or

Religious belief, or, worse still, superstition, and therefore is dismissed.

However, the fact remains that, in every culture in the world, highly revered and trusted Sages and Shaman have been saying for thousand years that we need only to 'believe' in order to see what our logical, rational mind cannot see.

Is it possible that we are prisoners of our own logical thought and belief system?

> "Until you experience something, it's one of those things where you have to show me the proof."
> **Erich Breger**

Brain Vision Filters

Our eyes, by nature, filter out about 80% of what is going on around us at all times. Our vision system is designed this way because it would be impossible to function if our brain had to process everything that is happening within our field of vision and awareness. To save processing power and be faster at identifying possible threats, our ego tells our brain to report only those movements that might evolve into a threat to our safety.

The part of our ego that is not our friend and wants to remain in control is not going to reveal things because our belief in spirits will result in the ego having less of a hold on us. Losing control over us is the one thing our ego is the most afraid of. Over our lifetime, our ego becomes a kind of runaway virus of the mind. (More on this topic in my book *'Your Worthiness Cycle'*)

Licking

Anyone who has had a cat knows what it feels like to be licked. A cat's tongue is very rough. It feels like someone is rubbing you with sand paper.

Mr. Zee took to licking the bottom of my feet and always in the same place... beneath my toes but above the arch of my foot, namely the pad of the foot, which is thicker to provide more protection when walking, running, etc.

He does this for several minutes in a row. It might be that he needs/wants the salt that is natural to the human skin. Perhaps he licks there because it has a thicker surface and he is trying to 'intake' some skin cells. Sucking on my toes might be drawing 'life force energy' from me so it is easier for him to manifest himself into a more 'alive' being. I have no idea but I have no doubt as to what he was doing.

My Thoughts, Feelings and Reactions

What am 'I' doing during these visits? What am I feeling, thinking, etc. Something about my approach to this has invited multiple vivid visits. If so, then it is quite possible that, by adopting some of the same thoughts, feelings and actions, you and others can have similar experiences.

Fear

My first reaction was that I was totally surprised, shocked and frightened. I thought it was Mr. Zee but I certainly was not 100 percent sure. Perhaps it was a tiger, or a snake, or a demon coming to get me and drag me into hell. Perhaps it was something that first appeared as Mr. Zee, and then turned into something scary once I lowered my defenses.

Mind

The first thing I realized was that I had to gain control of my fears. We experience fear physically, but its origins are in the mind. Fear does not actually exist. What we experience physically is the result of the fear of what we imagine might happen to us in the future.

The process for gaining control over our fear is to move from being a participant to being an *'observer.'* We begin by observing what is happening, rather than believing the scary stories that our minds dish out to us to feed the fear.

Here is just a sample of the thoughts that jumped up and demanded attention:

- I must be dreaming.
- I must be mistaken… this is not really happening to me.
- Something bad is about to happen.
- I am going crazy.
- I am *already* crazy, and now people are going to find out.
- I do not deserve to have this happening to me.
- I deserve every bad thing that could come of this.
- There is no such thing as a ghost/spirit. It's all in your head.
- Cats do not come back from the dead and neither does anything else.
- I should be doing something else right now that is much more productive.
- I'm hungry. I should get up right now and make something to eat.
- I need to go to the bathroom.
- I have an ache somewhere and need to attend to it.

A whole range of such bad, sad, scary, and ugly thoughts that all of us have stored in our minds presented themselves to me as possible explanations of what was happening.

I concentrated on staying calm. I reasoned that I was OK in the moment. I affirmed that I was in control of the situation. I could get up from the bed and turn the lights on any time I chose.

Body

The next I had to deal with was the tension in my muscles. Being tense would cause me to miss subtle movements and sensations. At the beginning of each visit, I would check my body and become aware of the degree of tension. I used self-talk to release the tension in each area of my body in a systematic way.

I also made a point of having a smile on my face and a positive attitude so I was giving off a 'positive vibe.'

> (One of the things I have spent some time learning about is the levels of consciousness and the resulting vibrations that all living things give off as explained in David R. Hawkin's book 'Power Versus Force.")

Almost from the beginning, I began to speak aloud to Mr. Zee. I told him that I was happy to have him there. I made sure to tell him that I knew it was him who was with me. I told him he was 'a good boy' which was one of our favorite communications when he was alive. I told him often that I loved him.

Breath

I tried to be very conscious of my breath. One of our natural reactions when we are afraid or excited is to hold our breath. While this helps us temporarily to notice subtle things easier, it soon has the affect of changing our brain waves, which then can play tricks on us. I noticed sometimes that if I held my breath, the movements he was doing seemed less pronounced. I discovered that the best way in the long run was to breath at a normal rate of about 15 – 20 full breaths per minute.

Stillness

I focused on being very still. I paid particular attention to any movements that I might unknowingly be making that could be causing those I was attributing to Mr. Zee.

No matter what he was doing or how uncomfortable something was, the longer I remained still, and just observed, the more I was assured that Mr. Zee wasn't doing anything that could do me harm. When I did move around, I did so slowly and deliberately, so as not to frighten him away.

Challenging the constant chatter of my mind required the most attention throughout this whole experience. Even without a ghost story attached, I believe it is the dominant challenge we have in every situation we find ourselves in throughout life.

Part VII - The Four Mouseketeers

Spring 2013 - Gina's Place

"If having a soul means being able to feel love and loyalty and gratitude, then animals are better off than a lot of humans."
~ James Herriot

One of my best friends ever was a fellow by the name of Dennis. We had met when I was just married.

Dennis had passed away three years earlier and it was one of the saddest times of my entire life. He was a true gentleman with more wisdom in his little finger than I have in my whole body.

I had spoken very little to his wife Gina since his passing.

My primary relationship at the time had ended, and I needed a place to stay for a few weeks while other accommodations were beginning made ready. I sent out an email to friends and family asking if anyone knew of a place I could stay at for a short while.

I was pleasantly surprised when Gina wrote back right away with an invitation to come and stay for as long as I needed. I was glad she did. My intuition had been telling me for a while that I should spend some time at her place. Since it was three years since Dennis's passing, I thought I might be able to help by doing some repairs or painting around the house.

Gina was Dennis's second wife. The day they met, they began a friendship , which had grown stronger every day of their two-decade marriage. I did not know for sure but I thought that Gina might be having quite a hard time letting Dennis go.

The second night of my stay, I had a visit from Mr. Zee, but this time it was very different. He still did his usual march from one side of my legs to the other, but he seemed to be a lot more heavy footed it did not make sense to me that Mr. Zee was getting heavier. As I paid closer attention, I realized that it didn't really feel exactly like that anyways. It felt more like something or 'someone' was pushing down on the mattress with each of Mr. Zee's steps.

After a couple of visits, I began to get a sense that it was my buddy, Dennis, who was pushing down on my bed. I wondered why he was still in the house. Was he trying to get my attention? For what reason? Then I realized that I might know the reason for his appearance.

There was another reason I was staying at Gina's home. A year and a half before Dennis died I had done something really stupid. It was nothing big but it was something where I owed Gina an apology. I was embarrassed and had kept my distance from these two wonderful people that I loved very much.

I knew Dennis had been sick. He had called me just before Christmas, a couple of months before he died. I did not call him back. (How many times do we make that mistake?) The next thing I knew, an email from Gina arrived late one night telling me that he had passed away.

I was completely devastated, not only because of his passing but because I had not stayed in touch and not done what I knew needed to be done.

I knew Dennis wouldn't have held any ill will against me because that was not who he was. I was fairly certain that Gina had no big negative charge on me either. Still, when we screw up with friends we have to make things right, within minutes if possible. Every minute we do not clear the air we create unnecessary misery for ourselves. This had not been a 'big deal' really. No sin had been committed but it had nagged me often over the previous three years.

The first few nights I was there, Gina and I talked about Dennis and what a wonderful person he was. There were lots of grins, giggles, belly laughs and more than a few tears from both of us.

Because I hadn't been there, I asked Gina if she would be so kind as to take me through the last year of his illness, and to share how she had been doing since. Then I did something that most people who know me will tell you is hard for me to do. I shut up and just listened.

Gina methodically recounted what had happened and shared her thoughts, feelings and how she was coping now.

I took a couple of days to think and feel my way through what she had told me, and then on the third evening I apologized for my insensitivity and plain lack of good manners. After admitting she had been pretty mad at me at the time, Gina accepted my apology with grace.

Why is this important to the story?

Mr. Zee visited a few more times before I moved back to the city. His 'heavy' footwork on the bed had disappeared and he was back being his ol' lighter self. The house seemed a bit fresher than it had been when I arrived.

Stories of people hanging around to make sure everything is OK have been told since the beginning or recorded history. These days, movies like 'Ghost' and 'Always' depict love stories between two people, each person in a different dimension.

However, there are a much greater number of movies whose sole purpose is to scare the living crap out of us (after we buy a ticket of course.) This is all done in good fun, but I do not think it is funny at all and never did.

Remember that song... *'If you're looking for trouble you've come the right place!'*

I think that in the realms of Ghosts and multiple dimensions of reality, if you are looking for trouble you are very likely to find it. I also believe that if you're looking for a love story, you will find that as well.

Belief, intent, need and expectation play a very important role in every aspect of our lives, but are *especially* important in this area. One of the reasons I believe that I have been honored with multiple visits, almost all of them positive, friendly experiences, is because I have enough training and awareness to keep these things in check.

With some awareness and concentration I have managed to:

- Not buy into *most* of the scary stories that forced their way to the surface of my mind.
- Not give too much energy to and the horror stories about 'what might happen next' that popped up out of nowhere.
- Remain open to a Truth beyond what I believe or do not believe.
- Be OK with not knowing, of residing in the Question instead of in the Answer.'
- Be careful not to make assumptions based on my beliefs.
- Not worry about what others believe or do not believe.
- Remain aware of my intention in each moment.
- Concentrate on the idea that there is a positive intention available and I can choose it.
- Believing that what ever or whomever visits, they have my best interests at heart and as I do theirs.
- Choosing to believe that I have enough power to attract a positive intention and co-create a positive outcome.
- Dig deep enough to make sure that the Intention I thought I was inviting was in fact, my true intention and not a disguised preparation for attack.
- Be careful not to *need* to see or have anything happen that would make the experiences more real.
- Be careful not to expect too much from the experience.
- Not need Mr. Zee to come, go or stay longer when he did come.
- Not need Mr. Zee to solve any of my current challenges.
- Not need him to make me happy, satisfied or fulfilled.

Summer 2013 - The RV Park

I returned to the city, and stayed with a friend at an RV Park while I was renovated my little retirement place.

The second night I was there Mr. Zee returned and came for several nights in a row. Things have evolved again. He was not even waiting until the lights were turned off, or for others to leave the room, before showing up.

The RV Park was the first time, since his initial departure from this earthly plane that Mr. Zee came to visit me in the daylight hours. I lay down for a nap one afternoon, and as soon as I pulled up a light cover, he was there.

Oh God, A Gaggle of Cats

Up until this point Mr. Zee had been visiting on his own. On occasion, I had wondered if there was more than one cat moving around.

On this particular night, he made his normal arrival around the foot of the bed and then settled on my left toe as his 'target du jour.'

Suddenly, I felt something moving around the bottom of my right foot, and then something else moving up my left side, and a fourth cat or spirit moving towards my right hand, which was above the covers.

Now, I understood the idea of Mr. Zee visiting. We were pals with a deep bond. But who else had he brought with him this time, and why? Was I about to be enveloped by a herd of cats biting, scratching and paying me back for all the times I wasn't home first thing in the morning to feed the King?

There was quite a bit of moving around for a minute or two, but then each of them headed to their respective corners. I was pretty sure it was Mr. Zee pushing on my right thumb. But who were these other characters? Were they new or duplicates, 'shadows of the shadows,' if you will.

One of them slowly made its way up to beside my left ear. This was the first time I had experienced a cat reaching all the way up to my head. It sat down beside my head, put its chin down on my shoulder and stayed there. Mr. Zee used to fall asleep with his head on my hand, (see picture) so I knew what it felt like, but to my recollection, he had never fallen asleep with his chin resting on my shoulder.

While this was happening, the fourth cat moved up my left side and stretched out leaning against my left side, level with my belly. I felt that it was facing towards my legs and was falling asleep there.

I could feel the warmth of one cat lying on my shoulder, and the warmth of the other cat lying at my left side. I could feel 'Zee Man' pushing my left thumb, and the whiskers of another cat gently moving back and forth against my right toe.

This went on for several minutes, until I felt myself falling asleep. Without being conscious of doing it, I started to roll over onto my left side. I don't remember what the other three were doing but the one that had been lying up close to my left side felt me rolling over and quickly 'got up' and scurried away so as not to get squashed.

This is important to note because the being was aware of me, aware of me making a move that would result in it ending up underneath me, and aware that it must move right away in order to be safe.

It follows that it must believe that it's 'alive' and has something to lose by being trapped underneath me, unable to move and perhaps unable to 'breath.' This raised the question, "Do Spirits need to breathe?"

October 30, 2013 - All Night Long

Many visits involved the same things so I began to only make a note when something out of the usual happened.

October 30 proved to be was another special night for our canine marauder.

I saw the covers the foot of the bed move this time, which I had not seen since the very beginning of his visits. It seemed that he was getting stronger and more 'real' over the course of the last few visits.

For the last few visits, Mr. Zee had been focusing on my big toes. He would still come up for a quick scratch on his chin, and then headed right back down to the toe. The drawing sensation was getting stronger with each visit. I wondered if he was drawing on my big toe to gather energy in some way.

(This was the first time I used my IPhone to record his movements in real time. I noticed that he did not stop, disappear, or even slow down when I was talking softly into my phone.)

Then Zee did something different. He wrapped his paws around my foot to steady it and make it easier to lick.

Miss Zulu Joins the Fun

Very soon after, another cat arrived at my other foot. I worried that there were going to be even more cats than before, but only those two came.

I got the idea that it might be our princess, Miss Zulu. Her arrival did not really surprise me. I had an inkling she would come eventually. Zulu seemed 'shy' but was following Zee's lead and began drawing on my other big toe for a minute or so.

I asked the Zeemeister out loud, "Is that Zulu who is with you? If so, come and get a scratch? I did not move my fingers or make any noise by scratching the blankets as I had always done. Mr. Zee stopped what he was doing immediately and quickly made his way up to my hand, which was waiting to give him his reward.

Right away, the new arrival began kneading the bed, which was a common thing for Zulu to do when she was alive. The purring from both of them became quite pronounced. While Zulu was kneading, Mr. Zee seemed to be taking delight in running his whiskers back and forth across the bottom of my foot and ankle. It seemed like some kind of celebration.

This carried on until around 5 am. I started to get tired, but the two of them were still 'doing their thing.'

By this time it was becoming a bit too much, so I got out of bed and put my socks on, and got back into bed. The only effect this had was to cause them to push a little harder on the bottom of my feet.

I finally drifted off, so I do not know when they actually left, but they were not there in the morning when I woke.

October 31, 2013 - The Two Z's

This is now the third night in a row that both of them have been with me. There are definitely two cats, not an echo of one, because they are doing different things at different times.

This night I left a light on so the room was lit, but only slightly. Once the two of them were happily sucking on my toes, I lifted the covers and held them aloft, while at the same time looking down towards the end of the bed. They didn't leave, but instantly made their way under the covers. They moved around a bit, but did not head back to my feet again until I had put the covers back to their normal place.

The previous night had been an 'all nighter.' I was tired and didn't want to be the center of attention once again. I think they must have felt my weariness, because they continued to lick the upper part of my feet, but in a gentle manner, without the intense sucking.

They continued to lick this padded area of my foot for some time, until I decided that enough was enough. This time, rather than putting my socks on I decided to try bending my knees and putting my feet flat on the mattress. I though this might be a way of telling them that I no longer wanted their attention.

They made their way up from the foot of the bed and walked around my feet and under my legs, which were now bent in a 'V' shape under the covers. Both of them were quite persistent. They tickled and pushed on my feet and rubbed up against my legs for a few minutes and then finally left. I was relieved when they did not return that evening, even after I put my legs back down and my feet back in their normal place.

November 1, 2013 - Something Cold

The two of them returned in their usual manner first one then the other. This time however the one that was learning against my right ankle suddenly became quite cold, very cold and it felt 'dark' for some reason. I did not like it much so I shook my leg and the cat and the cold feeling disappeared. Within a couple of minutes, a cat with the cold/dark feeling returned.

I was not comfortable with this cold sensation. I moved my leg out from under the covers and left it on top. The cold feeling went away except now my leg was no longer under the protection of the covers so it was getting chilled but not in the way you would expect. The chilled feeling was different from the cold feeling. It has never returned since that night

A Numb Thumb

I had been noticing for quite some time that the pads of my feet felt numb when I walked. Perhaps the constant licking by Mr. Zee and Zulu, with their rough cat tongues, is actually causing the pads of my feet to become thicker. Could it be that my feet were being gradually transformed into be more like cats paws?

I started to soak my feet and also to take more hot baths. The pads of my feet were thicker than normal but the skin easily softened and what didn't soften I removed with a brush made for that purpose. The numb feeling has been greatly reduced.

Not Tonight Zee, I Have a Headache

We were heading into another 'three nights in a row' and I was sick with the flu. I didn't want any sucking, licking, tickling from either of them. I was becoming irritated from too many long visits at once. Don't these guys ever sleep?" I wondered.

They both arrived as usual. I let the normal licking, etc. go on for a couple of minutes, but I knew I had to get some sleep. I put my feet flat on the mattress, and at the same time, I took both my hands out from under the covers and placed them beside me with fingers pointing up.

Immediately, they both stopped concentrating on my feet and moved up towards my hands, one on each side of my body. Soon they were sucking both my thumbs, and then one of them began to suck my index finger at the same time, and then the middle finger as well. My three fingers felt like they were being squeezed together and pushed on and twisted as animals do when they are trying to tear something apart.

The sensations were becoming intense to the point of hurting. "Maybe I am fooling around with something here I shouldn't be messing with. I decided to take this whole thing a little more seriously.

The feelings were so intense that I felt certain that I would be able to see them. I took a hard look at my hand where my three fingers were held tightly together. I saw nothing directly, but several times, I noticed movement out of the corner of my eye.

The sucking feeling became even more intense. I pulled my hands away, and waved my arms in the air, as if shaking them off. Then I slid my legs apart and together, as you do when you make 'snow angels.' It worked. They disappeared quickly, and did not return that night.

It seems I may have found a way to control how long they stay.

Looking For Patterns

With so many visits in a row, I was able to analyses what else was going on in my life. Had I drank any alcohol that night or the night before? Was I under or over tired? What TV shows had I been watching? What times had I gone to bed? Had I taken any medications? Had I eaten any particular type of food? How close was it to a full moon?

So far, the one thing that has been consistent is that nothing has been consistent. The visits happen in both the presence of one or more of the factors above and/or the absence of one or more.

- **Facebook.com/mrzeecomeshome**
- **Twitter - twitter.com/mrzeecomeshome**
- **YouTube - youtube.com/mrzeecomeshome**

Part VIII – More Extraordinary Every Day

December 9th – Sharing Energy

I do background acting for fun and profit. Yesterday I was on the set of '50 Shades of Grey' from 6:00 am in the morning until 8:00 pm at night.

For thirteen hours, two hundred of us were supposed to be in Savannah Georgia in the sunny month of May. What was really happening was that we were in Vancouver, mid December, in –7 degrees Fahrenheit, walking up and down a street with only summer clothes on, for hours, trying to look all warm, summery and happy. In addition, just to top it off there was a rain scene in the middle of the day, no less.

To say I was just a 'wee bit' fatigued is an understatement of the highest order. I was tired... Mr. Zee and Zulu were not. In fact, it seemed like they had been waiting for me all day because within three minutes of my pulling up the covers they had hopped up on the bed and were prancing around from my feet to my hands. They were really excited about something.

This was the first time that the two of them had arrived at the same time. They hopped up and made a beeline for my toes licking and sucking for all they are worth. One of them put their paws on a foot, one on each side of the foot and just held it.

Mr. Zee came up to my hand. First I felt his breath, then his whiskers and then he promptly wrapped his mouth around my left thumb and started to suck on it. I did feel his rough tongue this time as he was rubbing harder than ever.

I have always worried about letting the sucking go on too long. I have reasoned, although I don't know for sure, that he is drawing energy from me for himself, but I don't feel drained by it either at the end of the session or the next morning.

I never let it go on for more than five to ten minutes before stopping it by pulling my hand away, which always causes the sensation to disappear. If I put my hand back down on the covers again, he returns to his sucking within 30 seconds or so.

Last night I decided to let him go for as long as he wanted. I wanted to determine whether he would eventually be filled up by whatever it is that he was getting and would stop on his own. If he did get filled up, how long would it take before he was? Or would he just keep going? Would there be any noticeable residual feelings or any physical marks left in the morning if I let it go on for a long time?

Something seemed to be providing them with increased energy, allowing them to return more often, stay longer, and giving them more actual weight and presence as they moved around. The sucking seemed to be providing them with more physical strength as well.

After an hour he was still going, and it was getting uncomfortable, mostly because I had been holding my hand still for all that time.

When I got up in the morning there was no noticeable physical evidence. Nor did I feel I drained of anything, energetically or physically.

Having given up on the idea of getting a good night's sleep, I committed to discovering as much as I could. It became quite easy to determine which cat was which.

Zulu quite often makes her way up to my left groin area, lies down, starts to purr very softly for a few minutes, and then drops off to sleep. I can feel her weight lying on me, but once she is asleep, she does not move at all and stays in the same spot for a long time. I usually only notice her when I go to roll over at which point she wakes up and usually joins Mr. Zee, either at my feet or hands for a few minutes. Then she comes back and falls asleep again. This is very similar to when she used to lie on my lap when I was working on the computer. She did this the most when she had gotten sick and I was caring for her.

Zee, on the other, hand was a much larger cat. I can feel the difference in the depth of the depression they make in the mattress. I don't see the depression very often, only feel it, but there is a considerable difference between the two cats.

I had become accustomed to all the movements and sensations. I decided to start focusing on what was happening visually. With practice, would I be able to see a cat, parts of a cat or something else?

A Picture is Worth a Thousand Purr's

Looking straight at my hand as Zee sucked on it, I could see nothing. Gazing above or below him provided nothing, but the gazing provided a lot of half-second movements out of the corner of my eye. Several times I was sure I saw something white moving in my peripheral vision, either on one side or the other and sometimes both at the same time. As I said, my eyes are not the best, and fatigue in the middle of the night can do strange things to your head.

Last night I must have seen at least twenty movements, making it difficult to dismiss them all as illusions.

Having had so many possible sightings, I decided to see if I could get a picture of anything with my iPhone 4. I ended up taking about 150 shots. Some were above the covers; some were below. When I felt one or both cats really moving around, I snapped a picture in that general direction. Most of them I took with the flash. I tried some without the flash and I tried video as well.

The iPhone camera is quite slow. It also makes the sound of the shutter when you push the button. I attempted to turn off the sound so as not to give these two characters any advanced warning but could not find a way to do it at the time.

Miss Zulu Appears

Halfway through the night, still nothing. I had probably taken a hundred shots by that time. I then tried a number of shots in a row as fast as the iPhone would take them. The originals show that they are numbered sequentially, and that they were all taken at 1:05 am. I estimate about 1 second apart. They have been sized to fit on the following page, but other than that, they have not been retouched in any way. The bright spot at the top right of the central picture is my finger. The white fluffy thing in the middle of the picture look as though it could be Miss Zulu sitting between my legs, pointed away from me. The picture below the three is the same as the one in the middle one, only larger

Is this Miss Zulu in the middle of the photograph?

December 13th - Intense Activity

There has been intense activity over the last 3-4 days.

I now have discovered that there are two groups, one made up of Zulu and Mr. Zee and the other made up of less evolved beings

With both Zulu and Zee, there is an actual weight against my body. I feel my body heat being reflected back to me. Both of them start to purr within a minute of settling down and continue until they leave or I fall asleep. They both have favourite spots that they go to often.

There are at least three different cats that have visited but usually only one or two of them visit at one time. They seem to be smaller and act like kittens but I don't think they are either Zulu's or Mr. Zee's kittens. Neither of them had babies when they were alive.

The Spirit cats are very active. They appear and disappear at various places around my body. They seem to have little mass. I have felt whiskers and tails but not much else.

Zulu and Zee have a relationship with me, which they are maintaining in the ways described above. The others just want to feed.

They arrive. First, I feel whiskers on my skin and then they go directly to either my toes or my fingers and attempt to latch on. They move up and down my hand or foot until they reach the toes/fingers and start to lick the ends. I can feel their tongue on my skin.

Very quickly however, they begin to surround the finger with their mouth. As the sucking intensifies in pressure, they move farther onto my finger working their way to my knuckle and beyond. If I allow it, more than one will latch onto other fingers on the same hand. So far, I have had as many as three on the same hand.

At first, this was OK but over time, it has gotten a lot stronger to the point where the sucking has become quite uncomfortable. I used to be able to just pull my finger away a little bit and the sensation would stop but last night two of them had latched on my index and middle finger on my right hand. I moved my hand around to gain a release but they stayed attached. I moved a little farther and still they stayed attached. I finally had to shake my hand rapidly to get to release at which time they disappeared and did not return that night.

They are very persistent. I will shake the covers and/or move my arms in the air or swish my legs back and forth to get ride of them and they will disappear but often reappear within half a minute or so. They almost always return to the location where they were at before my attempt to have them release.

At first, I didn't notice any residual sensation from the sucking but after a few sessions, I began to notice that it makes my fingers/toes numb if I allow it to go on too long.

A few days later, I am noticing that the numbness is still there in the morning. The index and forth finger on my left hand were completely numb when I awoke and continued to be for an hour. There is a slight sensation of the fingers being slightly burned, as if I had put the tips of my fingers around a hot cup of coffee.

December 20th - Moving Beyond The Bed

In the last few days, one of them has taken to sucking at other locations. It has located a place on the upper outside of my left leg just above the ankle. It doesn't feel like it has latched onto anything but rather like it is just placing its mouth on my leg. It doesn't lick or suck but is very persistent so it must be getting something from that location. I have attempted to shoo it away but it mostly returns to that same location. This does not happen every night but the location is the same.

A couple of times there has been a quick sharp jab that made me jump. It didn't feel anything like knife or a needle being inserted, but more like a jab with something very thin, like a mosquito bite only with a longer stinger. There was no swelling or red mark the following morning and the spot did not itch.

All activities at every visit up until now have happened while I am in bed but lately I am starting to feel them around my feet when I'm sitting at a table or watching TV. I feel something brush against my foot and look but nothing is there. I am feeling it a few times each night.

Last night I was sitting in a recliner watching TV. I had my runners on and one of them was pulling on the side of it, trying quite intensely to pull the runner off my left foot. I had my left leg crossed over my right one. There was a loose thread attached to the runner moving back and forth, but it seemed to be out of focus when I looked at it. The thread was moving like it was blowing in a light breeze.

Hey, There's An App For That

Doing research on the Internet I discovered that there are 'ghost detector' apps available for smartphones. These are often abbreviated versions of equipment used by professional paranormal investigators.

I downloaded several from the iTunes and tested them individually over several nights. Some are just for fun, probably designed to 'make stuff up' so you can scare the daylights out of your friends. Others are complete hoaxes. I did locate three that gave me readings that made sense.

One app in particular worked very well. It is like a radar screen with circles, sections and quadrants. It gives off a blip whenever it identifies an anomaly in the EMF (Electro Magnetic Field).

I sat up in bed and placed the iPhone down in my lap. There were no lights or electronic devices on in the house. All computers were turned off to reduce electronic interference as much as possible. This proved to be unnecessary as the software seems to measure what is constant within its range and filters it out.

I would feel a movement on the outside of my left leg and a blip would show up on the app in that general location. I would feel it moving towards me and the blip would move in the same direction. Sometimes I would get the blip first before I felt a movement and other times after the movement. If I were feeling three on the bed, I would most often get three (or more) blips on the screen. Sometimes the blip would stay for a minute or so and other times it would disappear quickly. Many times, there were blips on the screen when I did not feel any movement at all in that general direction. The readings were consistent after several tests over several days. The app doesn't tell you much, but what it does tell you is quite accurate. More on this later once I learn how all this stuff works.

Seeing Really is Believing

With the iPhone, I have more evidence as to how many cats are participating in the day's activities. I have strong indication as to 'where' some of them are at any particular time.

This new tool justifies spending more time trying to 'see' these beings.

As I mentioned before, I have often seen movements out of the corner of my eye but only for half a second and when I looked directly at where the movement was coming from there was nothing.

Doing more research, I learned that we see more out of the corner of our eye because the edges of our eyes are more sensitive to and pick up more light. We are designed this way for survival. The sooner we see danger coming at us in our peripheral vision the sooner we can respond. Perfectly logical.

To see the things flashing around in the corner of your eye the technique is to stay looking forward but actually 'see' what is going on out of the corner of your eye. Once something moves you have to resist the impulse to change your stare from straightforward in the direction of where you identified the movement. It takes some practice. It is not just visual. This new skill involves new programming and wiring between your eye, brain and muscles so you will not see it 'until you do.' Have a positive result once and, like riding a bike, the rest is just practice. For lack of a better term I will call this 'Side View Looking."

First Sighting

Last night again I was not concentrating on seeing anything. I was certain that Zulu was at my left side and the closest to my face.

Zulu and I had also been bonded although she was more Tanis's cat. I communicated with her by speaking and making loving sounds and her communications were by blinking and purring. She knew the feeling that were associated when I said, "I love you", or "You're a beautiful girl", "my little princess. "I had developed a special sound just for her when she was alive that sounded kind of like a bird cooing.

I started to say our favourite phrases and make loving sounds in the tone she would likely recognize.

I thought I spotted the shape of her head sitting up and looking at me so I attempted to look at her using the Side View Looking technique. After a couple of minutes which involved several reboots of the Side View technique I saw the distinct features of her head but then couldn't' resist moving my eyes towards her at which point she completely disappeared. OK, back to step one. Once I ran the program in my head, again a few times I was able to see what I had seen before only this time it was a lot more vivid.

Zulu remained a type of shadow. There was nothing 'solid.' I could make out her features enough that I felt certain it was Miss Zulu. She was dull grey in color, which would have translated into white in the proper light. She was looking around, turning her head, back and forth, in a relaxed manner. I would feel the sensation of her center of balance changing as she turned her head and leaned a little more on one foot than the other. I was able to correlate those sensations with visual observation. When she bent down to sniff, I felt her whiskers on my skin. When she lifted her head the whisker feeling disappeared.

From then on it became easier and easier to see as long as I followed the Side View Looking process. Concentration is very important. Without maintaining a high level of concentration your brain will instinctively tell your eyes to move towards the object at which point you lose sight of it and have to reboot the eye/brain process to see these subtle energy's again. Our brain will also try to get our eyes to focus on the subject whereas maintaining a gaze slightly out of focus is how you will get the best results.

A few times, I looked down towards my right foot where Zee was moving around. I could see something very transparent but not well as he was farther away and I would have had to reposition my body to get a better view. This would have disturbed Zulu so I decided to attempt to see him at another time.

Stop The Sucking Will Ya Please

The sucking by the kittens was getting to be too much of a good thing but 'for them,' not me. I was worried that if I fell asleep they would all latch on at once and then God knows what might happen. Would I have any fingers left in the morning? Would my hands now have hair growing out of them? I did not know and I really did not want to find out.

Searching the Internet for things to discourage them, I found all kinds of suggestions on Forums about getting rid of Ghosts and Spirits. Here are only a few:

1. Leave a candle burning. (Didn't make any difference)
2. Wear garlic. (Rubbing garlic oil on my legs helped.)
3. Use various essential oils (None I tried had any affect.)

What I did find that worked was to put a few drops of Oil of Oregano on each foot and a few on the tips of my fingers. That night the kids did not know what to do. They would come up looking for some of my finger candy and then back away, then attempt a few times more before losing interest. The next night I tried it again and for most of the night only Zee and Zulu were on the bed which was a nice break in the action.

Please help Mr. Zee and Allan get the word out

Review *'Mr Zee Comes Home'* on Amazon

http://bit.do/MrZeeReviews

Part IX – Back To The Future

> *The more enlightened our houses are, the more their walls ooze ghosts.*
> ITALO CALVINO, The Literature Machine

At the end of Part IV, I posed a number of questions? I have not made extra effort to answer these questions directly. I hope that the story I am telling as honestly as I know how to do will provide YOU with the answers that resonate with you.

In trying to understand why all this has been happening I first have to ask myself: What have I done/not done, if anything, to encourage and/or facilitate this happening. I am not aware of doing/not doing anything deliberately, so by deductive reasoning, I did or not do some thing or things for other reasons that somehow combine to open a portal to these experiences.

The quote above suggests that I might consider myself enlightened but nothing could be further from the truth. Believe me, besides Zee and Zulu I have a few more ghosts taking up space in my head. I have fears, doubts, regrets, resentments and many things that I have not forgiven others or myself for.

There are a few of my past experiences that might have prepared me for Mr. Zee's and Company's three and a half years of visits and communications.

Some of the people I have been exposed to, along with their teachings and beliefs, most likely have had an impact. Finally, some of the things I have chosen to believe and how I view Belief itself is an important enough factor to dig into a little deeper.

Our past always is affecting our present. The best we can hope for in life is that things from our past will not also have too much of an impact on our future.

Past Experiences

Originally, I didn't think I had any experience that would predispose me to communicate with Mr. Zee. However, as I worked back through my life, I remembered things that could have led me subconsciously to a state of acceptance of spirits, ghosts and other paranormal experiences.

(This is probably the first reason this happens to people. They become willing to accept that things like this can, and will, happen.)

Georgie, The Human Vacuum Cleaner

In the mid 90's, I hooked up with a healer from Toronto by the name of Georgie. I was on the road doing a series of seminars on Worthiness and Georgie attended my presentation at the Omega Center.

Afterwards Georgie wanted to take me for coffee and pick my brain about Worthiness and other mutual interests. She was delightful, a total sponge to my conversation. Never let anyone listen to your every word and look at you with sexy eyes. By the next morning, we were partners, both in the 'biblical' sense and in business.

We started with me doing the public seminars and Georgie doing the individual counseling sessions with those that felt they needed more after the seminar.

Georgie was a Czechoslovakian Jew whose father had been a high level Rabbi in the old country. She had trained at the Edgar Cayce Institute in guess what... Spirit Releasement Therapy, of all things. This was a million miles from my belief system at the time but I came to appreciate her and her work very much.

People would come to her home. After asking the client what they felt was wrong she would identify the type of spirit and what it looked like to her. Then, after laying them down on her massage table, she would put her hands on the areas where the 'stuck energy' had been located and make, first a sucking sound through her teeth and then a burping, belching sound, which was to get rid of whatever it was she had pulled out of the patient.

Reportedly, some would be just little blobs of light like what is known as an Orb. Others came in all shapes and sizes, including that of a black snake that Georgie said would coil around some part of the body and was holding on for 'dear life.' Some were positive and happy, some were unhappy and some were dark. Although some quite resistant, none were able to remain with the right treatment. I wondered if some were dangerous to their host and to the practitioner.

"Aren't you afraid that they will come out of the patient and get stuck inside of you? "I asked.

"Not at all," Georgie reported. "Learning how to not get hooked into that particular story is what they teach you at the Edgar Cayce Institute."

Georgie would prepare herself by putting a bubble of light around herself for protection. She would then ask for and receive the support of the Universe. Ready to proceed she would ask the stuck energy what it needed. Once that was determined, Georgie would just 'love' it until the unwelcome spirit released itself from the subject. As the final step she would then bless them send them on their way into the light.

Georgie explained to me that all 'aberrations' are really pieces of Light, of various degrees of intelligence, who are mostly lost, stuck between this world and the next. All they really want is return to the energy/light/heaven. It was beyond what my 'red neck, prairie boy' belief system could handle at the time, but I saw first hand how many of her clients gained comfort and freedom from her work. She was very busy with a full practice so who was I to judge? We worked together for several months. I am most grateful to Georgie because she opened my eyes to things I had resisted and rejected. The result was a major growth spurt for me.

Just Visiting, Not Attached

I am not sure if this applies to Zee and Zulu. They seem to be content to sleep on my bed and hang out for the rest of the day doing whatever it is that Spirits do. In reading reports of other pets who have returned (see the website: MrZeeComesHome.com). I find that pets often fall into their regular routine after they return. They are not officially 'stuck' but rather choose to come back just to be around and do what pets do. I never sensed any frustration or pain coming from Zulu or Mr. Zee so I didn't really feel the need to do anything in terms of encouraging them to go.

Clearing The Mind

One thing I have no doubt plays a factor in having these experiences, is the ability to clear the mind and keep it clear.

I have had a passion for self-help and personal growth since I was very young. I read my first self-discovery book when I was eleven. It was called "*How to Hypnotize Yourself.*" I have joked many times that it must have worked because I spent the next thirty years 'un-hypnotizing' myself.

Having been involved in personal development both my own and professionally for more than forty years, I have had the privilege of working directly with some amazing professionals in the field. Folks like Zig Ziglar, Dennis Waitley, John Bradshaw, Don Beck, Tony Robbins to name only a few.

The guy that took me the farthest in terms of inner healing and spirituality is Dr. Chuck Spezzano.

Chuck travels the world doing deep process healing workshops and teaching a very in-depth model of consciousness called 'The Psychology of Vision'. His work contributed significantly to my understanding of Worthiness, which is my specialty.

The key and deeper purpose of any body of work in the self development is to learn how to do two things:

1. Clear the mind of judgments, projections and misinterpretations that are lodged within and holding us back from our potential.
2. Learn how to open up to include more truths in order to form a higher Truth, more in line with our potential. (I call this Inclusionism)

Doing both of these things clears the way for us to be able to be more of who we really are and be able for us to deliver our own unique gifts into the world.

Seeing Aura... No Big Deal

"You can't be critical, analytical in your investigation if you don't leave room for doubt. You can't think you know everything."
~ **Claudia Metz**

I had never seen an aura so I did not know whether they were real or the result of some really good drugs back in the 60's. Most of the self-help stuff I had studied to any degree was about either character development and/or performance improvement. I had stayed away from what I call the *'booga booga'* stuff as much as possible.

For some reason, most of my friends were 'believers' of such heady things as The Soul, the Afterlife, and Multiple Dimensions of Reality. I always listened to their stories, learning's and beliefs but secretly felt that I was indeed the *'superior one'* because I had evolved myself beyond all this myth, folklore and suspicions.

Spezzano opened my knowingness to the hundreds, if not thousands or layers of the mind, each releasing more of our true potential.

The easiest thing I ever did was see an aura... no big deal... one day I just looked at someone who was sitting in front of me in a room and there it was. Actually, I didn't know what it was at first. I strained my eyes to see what I thought was the glare of the neon lights above but no... holly gobs of plasma batman... there it was... an aura in all its splendor.

It was even more startling to me because I was seeing this energy field around a gal named Beverly, who was someone I was not particularly fond of... no, I'm being too kind... someone I didn't like at all. I thought of her as someone who would not have an aura even if they actually existed. My head had reasoned that it should have made it harder if not down right impossible for me to acknowledge and identify her 'life force' and the total innocence that she was, is and will always be.

Cleaning Out Head... A Very Big Deal

Now... the HARDEST thing I ever did was go through the three days from early morning to late into the nigh, clearing my mind of all the junk buried there, in order for me to actually see that aura.

I was participating in a workshop designed to help clear the mind of all the layers of hurts, disappointments and emotional wounds that we all end up with sooner or later.

> (This workshop was facilitated by Sandy Levey, who is one of the originators of 'The Clearing Process' and Duane O'Kane, founder of the ClearMind Institute of Vancouver BC. Both these individuals are highly qualified and continue to help people clear themselves of the thoughts from the past that bind them, so that they can have a fresh future.

All these wounds require 'healing' which is to say identified, processed and released so that we can become more of the person we actually are without all these burdens attached. The result of a clear mind is to be able to access power that is more personal, intuition, and resiliency. From there, the benefits are more Happiness, Success and Fulfillment. Clearing our mind allows us to be able to include more of everything in our thinking without losing ourselves in the process. This includes more of things unknown including the paranormal.

All roads lead to Rome and, as such, there are many different processes to help us achieve a clearer mind. The Spezzano process has four steps:

1. Understanding
2. Acceptance
3. Forgiveness
4. Letting Go

Understanding – This is the realization that if we *really* understood, why our mother, father or other perpetrator (and their ancestors) behaved the way they did with us, we would be released from the trap of thinking they did it to us *personally*. Spending time understanding people's motivations at the subconscious level causes us to grow internally.

After helping over 100,000 people over 35 years, Chuck claims that when you make the investment in expanding your thinking in order to understand what happened, about 60% of the charge we have on these people, the events that caused the wound, and the situations we ended up in as a result are released from our body, mind, and heart.

Acceptance – We gain back more personal power when we accept things as they are. We accept others, and, most importantly, we accept ourselves.

The movie *"A Prince of Tides"* was particularly important to me. I probably watched it 30 times or more. Although I did not have anything near as horrific happen to me as what happened to Tom Wingo (played by Nick Nolte) the results have been more or less the same.

In the beginning of the movie, Tom is doing a narrative introducing the story:

> "From my mother, I inherited a love of language… and an appreciation of nature. She could turn a walk around the island into a voyage of purest discovery."

> "As a child, I thought she was the most extraordinary woman on earth."

> "I wasn't the first son to be wrong about his mother."

> "I don't know when my parents began their war against each other."

> "But I do know the only prisoners they took were their children."

At the end of his opening narrative he says:

> "All this was a long time ago… before I chose not to have a memory."

That last line shook me to my core. Although I had been reading and speaking about self help for many years by that time that line was really the beginning of my journey 'back to myself.'

At the end of the movie, he speaks of Acceptance. He has found his way back to himself:

> "It is in the presence of my wife and children... that I acknowledge my life, my destiny.
>
> I am a teacher... a coach... and a well-loved man. And it is more than enough.
>
> In New York, I learned that I needed to love my mother and father... in all their flawed, outrageous humanity. And in families... there are no crimes beyond forgiveness."

Acceptance is not so much that you accept that people are who they are even if they are wrong. We accept the idea that 'all things happen for a reason.' We can learn valuable life lessons from everything that happens and 'we are 100% responsible for the progress or lack thereof that we make in our lives afterwards.

Forgiveness – Sir John Templeton, was one of the wealthiest people on the planet. When he retired, he invested over $40 million dollars in a research study on Forgiveness.

Simply put, the results of the research demonstrated that Forgiveness is the healthiest thing we can ever do for ourselves. It actually facilitates physical as well as mental healing. It frees us to be the person we are capably of being and achieve levels of success, happiness and fulfillment we would have never dreamed possible. But, and it is a big 'but,' forgiving is one of the hardest things that human beings ever do. In fact, at the deeper levels of the mind, it is probably *the* hardest thing we ever do, until it .

If we were designed like a computer we would just log on, move some files (memories) around that should be stored under a different category, then re-valuate what was necessary and valuable for our future survival and delete the rest. 'God don't make no mistakes' but he could have saved us all centuries of misery if she had made this feature standard equipment.

There are skills and techniques that can be learned quite easily if we make the investment. But, and here's the other big 'but,' our lower mind is very good at convincing us that revenge, resentment and judgments are far better to hold on. It is the biggest lie we allow our minds to convince us. Regardless, learning, knowing and integrating all-important Truths takes some real effort and commitment on our part.

> *"Forgiveness is giving up all hope of having had a better PAST."*
> ~ Anne Lamott

Letting Go – Coming in a close second on the 'hard to do for humans', scale is letting go of the stories, beliefs and judgments about ourselves and others that hold us back. Some of us hold onto them so that we will see them coming next time and therefore will be able to survive the present and future. *'Survive'* is the operative word here because if we don't let go of the judgments we have on others and most importantly, ourselves, we will do just that… survive. Judgments help to keep us safe but nothing about judgments will ever allow us to be happy or fulfilled. "Judgment perpetuates a self-fulfilling prophecy that always brings us back to where we feel we are safe. Nothing about judgment includes abundance."

Another way to describe a judgment is anything that we need to be right about. "We say in relationship counseling: *"You can be right or you can be happy but you can't be both!"*

Ironically, as it turns out, we hold on because we are afraid of the Light more than the Dark. By its nature, the future is unknown. In order to mitigate our fear of the unknown, the unexpected and being overwhelmed by too many good things happening at once, we hold onto the frightening past because it is less frightening than the future. In reality then, we use our past to protect us from the future and the possibility of more Success, Happiness and Fulfillment.

Deepak Chopra says that we think about 60,000 thoughts a day. That is a bunch. The sad news is that about 95% of those thoughts are the same as we thought yesterday. Many of those are debates and arguments we are still having with people years after the original event that resulted in the original grievance. Some of the arguments we are having are with people who have long since died. Is it any wonder we are not as creative as we feel we can be? Is it any wonder we feel fatigued so often or have trouble getting to sleep at nights?

I could go on for another hundred pages or so but the point is that without doing some of this work you are not likely to experience cats jumping up on your bed or many other things that would add greater richness to your life.

Trees Have Auras Too

A few years later, I was at Ships Point Bed and Breakfast on Vancouver Island. I had been hired by a couple to help them get their relationship back on track. This was it. Divorce court was the next stop if we were not successful this weekend in getting this couple turned around.

I had been facilitating the clearing process (as taught by Sandy Levey) with this couple. I was not actually working at clearing my own mind but helping them to clear themselves of judgments and grievances, first with each other and then with each of themselves personally. (At the end of the day, I believe all clearing is about us and with us.) There is no 'out there' but only our own experience of our own consciousness.

At about 2:00 pm I called for a break and the three of us took a walk along the beach. At the end of the path, there was a small track of old growth forest. Only a few feet into the forest, I realized I could see the energy/aura of every tree. At this level of the mind, everything is alive and speaks to you as a feeling or knowingness. Each tree was broadcasting something a little different. I didn't hear any actual words. Rather each tree provided me with a 'sense' of what it wanted me to know. The whole experience was remarkable. Very inspiring!

Understanding Belief

In our world we are programmed mostly 'not to believe.' That programming causes us to put walls up to protect ourselves from things that are manufactured by someone else. We end up shadow boxing with illusions we have been told were real by others.

It can be said that when we believe nothing (what Landmark calls Empty and Meaningless) we can know everything but while believing that knowing everything is a good thing, it is a belief we need to transcend as well.

Beliefs we have adopted that has been provided by others gets in the way of us seeing many things that would move us forward.

Hollywood has shaped our perception to sell seats in movie theaters.

Our education system with its scientific based bias either does not discuss paranormal events at all, or demands proof. We all have been educated in a *'If I see it I'll believe it' system*.

Many religions haven't helped much either, insisting that any paranormal experience has to be either Christ, an angel, a fallen angel, a demons or even worse... Satan himself in disguise.

This book reports what I personally, with a clear mind, have experienced. To some, this recounting is an assurance of things they already believed to be true. Others will need more proof than I or anyone else can provide.

Needing Proof

The difference between *Assurance* and *Proof* is that Proof is a *'Yes/No'* full stop process. Either you believe it, or you do not. There is no 'almost' true. Seeking proof requires us to make a judgment. Judgments always come from a hard point, whereas Assurance is more gentle. Seeking assurance rather than proof allows us to slide in beside something, for a while, to expand our understanding of it and all its nuances.

To remove any doubt resulting from poor writing or explanation here are the facts as I state them in this book:

- Everyone in this book is a real person or animal. I have used the actual first name of each person, unless asked to do otherwise.
- The events told throughout this book happened to me personally. It is a first hand accounting.
- Although I had to move a few things around slightly for clarity, the events in the book happened in the order in which I have presented them.

The happenings, events and encounters reported here are presented as accurately as my memory and experience can provide. Where something happened that I do not have a clear recollection of, I say so at that point in the book.

Holding Fast To What We Believe.

"I simply don't' believe in any of this stuff."

I get it and my former self could not agree with you more. Most readers will be skeptical. Please be skeptical. That's OK. I won't take it personally. We are all conditioned repeatedly to be skeptical, doubtful and cynical. That is simply human nature and not a bad thing at all. In the time of Socrates, being a skeptic was not considered to be a negative. Skeptic simply meant to be someone 'who keeps on asking questions and resisting coming to a conclusion.'

Belief is dynamic. Some of the things I believed last week I no longer believe because I have received new information. It would be foolish to ignore new information as it offers new opportunities that I never would have been aware of before. We humans have always evolved in our beliefs. We would not have survived as long as we have if we were not very good at changing, adapting and evolving our beliefs.

Bare in mind, many people and institutions discourage us from evolving our beliefs. To surrender our beliefs to others, including those that helped us form those beliefs in the first place is to give 'power to others over us' which eventually costs us much in terms of awareness, understanding and expansion.

A New Way to Look at Belief

Consider this. Let us say you and I have a belief, one single belief. I believe that this belief is 100% true. You on the other hand believe that it is 0% true.

Between 0% and 100%, there is a half way point, which is of course is 50%. In order to evolve our belief system we have to move towards that which we <u>do not</u> believe. This is true of any and all beliefs between any two people or group.

The 50% line is not a compromise because it is fifty percent of the whole Truth along the full spectrum of that belief. Therefore, the only way to fully evolve and grow is to be willing to include all of the 'other' 50% into our belief system. This is the only choice other than standing at our point on the spectrum and refusing to move. To fully evolve we must travel that path. Your 50% is the distance I need to travel to be fully satisfied, assured, confident and legitimate and mine is yours.

I have also come to know (begrudgingly) that *'just because I don't' believe something does not mean it isn't true.*

More Connection is Always Possible

I have invested these many words in this chapter to explain one reason why I believe I am able to receive Mr. Zee's visits. I certainly don't claim to have a clear mind all the time or am more clearer than anyone else. I do think that the processes and techniques I learned, in order to get clear, have removed enough of the 'trance' we live in for me to experience a more direct connection with the unseen Mr. Zee. I have noticed that the more time I invest in being clear the more often he is wiling and/or able to visit.

Mr. Zee and I doing an interview on my radio show.

Part X - Worthiness: The Key To Everything

I do not know all of the reasons why Mr. Zee returns, but I know one thing for sure. Worthiness has something to do with it.

Congratulations, by the way, for reaching this far in the book. Seeing ghosts is a juicy topic, but understanding and using what you are about to learn is the juiciest of all. This next section can literally change your life for the better in many significant ways.

I have been researching Worthiness since 1995. Events in my life at that time caused me to question the whole concept of self-esteem, self worth and self-acceptance. I began to feel that the definitions of these important life-defining, life-changing concepts, and the way we go about improving our self esteem/self-worth, was limited, inadequate and, in some ways, simply wrong.

The fact is, there is a much deeper and much more relevant dynamic impacting the degree of success, happiness and fulfillment we achieve in our life. I call this dynamic *'Worthiness.'*

One of the reasons we have not been able to make any great strides in the areas of self-esteem and self-worth is that they are all explained using words only. They are concepts, part of an overall philosophy of self-improvement which, at its core, tells us that we are fundamentally flawed and we must do something about it.

Researching self-worth, I eventually came to the conclusion that what we call self-worth is a measurement we use to measure ourselves against other people and things in the world. It is a completely bogus assessment. In truth, we are each as valuable as any other. Yes, we as humans place more value on some people than others, but very few of those people whom we place a higher value on would claim to be more valuable than anyone else.

Oprah, a multi-billionaire, explained this well on 'Larry King Live.'

(Paraphrased) "My so called riches, money, fame, success, and possessions don't make me one cent more valuable than anyone else. They only provide me with the means to do more for others. Anyone giving of themselves and their resources is just as valuable as my giving. Having the means to give more to more people does not add any special value to my giving. I do not earn one pass for my sins and not one extra point for my achievements. We're all the same in God's eyes."

We have infinite value, we are all completely, and totally, '*innocent' no matter what we have said or done.* This is easier to accept at the 'Observer' level, the 'God' level, if you will. I believe we are all completely innocent, because at the 'God' level of things all of what and why everything happens is observable. From that vantage point of awareness, we can know the past, present and future of everyone and everything involved.

In his book "Paranormal" Dr. Raymond Moody, creator of the terms 'near death experiences' and 'afterlife,' says that one common experience reported by those that have died and come back is that they go through a life review. However, it is nothing like what we've been told it is, the much feared 'Judgment Day."

As reported by tens of thousands of people, the life review is witnessed from a place of non-judgment and love. It is as if you are being shown how, if you had known better, you would have done it differently. You did not know what you know now, so you are assured that you are completely innocent.

The term "sin" as it was originally used was an archery term that mean simply to 'miss the mark, probably because in Latin 'sinister' means "on the left." The left-handed were considered "sinister" because they were more likely to "miss the mark!"

Sin, to my way thinking is not a sin at all, but rather just a mistake. A mistake can be corrected. We can change our way of thinking and our behavior to something that is more in integrity for us, and of more service to others. Accepting that we are completely innocent, no matter what we have done, said or thought is a major step forward in our development. Once accepted we can also accept that we have things stored up inside us that cause us to not 'feel' innocent. To get closer to the truth we need only move those things aside and release them.

I had many questions. When we say we have "low self-esteem," what unit of measurement are we using to arrive at that conclusion? Low compared to what? If it is low now, where did it start? How low can our sense of self-esteem or self worth go? How high can it get? Most importantly, how do I change its current direction from heading lower to improving and rising higher? How do I do this sooner, faster and with less work and struggle?

I came to the conclusion that what was needed was a visual model so that we could 'see' what self-esteem, self-worth and authentic worthiness look like. We learn about 80% of what we know from visual observation. Words alone can end up just swirling around in our head, causing us confusion and lack of direction.

In this visual model, I have placed 'Worthiness' on a simple graph of a cycle representing the rise and fall of our ability to repel and release that which is negative, and to accept more and more of what is positive.

We all have 'ups and down's throughout our entire life. All of us at some point or the other feel like we are on a wild roller coaster ride. For others it is a slight rise and fall and rise again that never gets beyond the highest point we've ever experienced in life.

Worthiness Explained

Our Worthiness is made up of two distinct elements, which are almost opposites, but not quite.

One side of the Worthiness equation is *'being able to withstand.'* When we say a bridge is worthy, we mean that the bridge is able to withstand the weight of all the vehicles that are going to pass over it, as well as any strong winds, floods, earthquakes, etc. This half of the Worthiness equation is about resiliency. Not only will the bridge withstand what comes at it today, but for many decades to come. We must learn how to withstand all that comes at us in life. We must be resilient enough that we don't allow these things to drive us lower and lower until we 'hit bottom' and/or leave this earth 'with our music still in us' which I call *'Nothing.'*

In our western construct of reality, we emphasize and promote this aspect of Worthiness to the expense of all others. Our collective mantra is:

'Be strong', *'go for it'*, *'Win'*, *'if you want it you have to go out and get'*, *'you have to take what you want in life because nobody (or no thing) is going to hand it to you on a silver platter.'*

The other aspect of Worthiness is more important. In fact, it is the most important of all. It is a way of being where we are able to 'relax, release, attract, accept and receive in abundance all the good things that come (and want to come) to us in life.'

In the beginning of our *'Receiving'* some of what comes our way is because of all the hard work we did when we were out 'getting'. We must, almost completely switch the way we view this, to learn how to *'allow ourselves to receive with* ease' every good thing that comes at us. Once learned, we must then learn to allow and receive even more in greater quantity, quality and intensity. This process never stops no matter what level we are at.

Now you will begin to understand why healing, releasing and personal transformation beyond the things we 'think and feel' we are guilty of is so important. You can have negative beliefs about yourself and still go out in life driving yourself as hard as you can to achieve success. However, when you start receiving you will discover that you very quickly rise to a point where you are always 'at the train station when you're ship comes in' because secretly you feel you do not deserve it. Our resistance to the *'good'* is definitely the biggest secret we keep from ourselves and others. This goes for financial wealth, relationships, career, health and everything else.

Most people know how to work hard and be constantly trying to improve their performance and productivity. Almost as many fail to recognize that there are many times (often moment by moment) to make the switch to 'allowing.'

Our parents, educations system, and our culture do not provide the education , understanding and/or skills for us to learn how to keep allowing and receiving no matter how good it gets. I used to have a radio program called *"How Good Can You Stand It?"* which is one of the most important questions you need to as yourself and keep asking yourself every day.

There are terms we use for people who learn the 'going out and getting' part. We call them' real fighters, drivers, achievers and winners.' Nothing wrong with that at all, but there is so much more available. For people who learn the 'allowing' aspect of Worthiness as well we use those same words but we add on a few more like Happy, Peaceful, Successful, Accomplished, and Fulfilled.

At our deepest level, we are constantly trying to learn both of these aspects of Worthiness because, it will allow us to reach higher than what we will ever thought possible.

What becomes the major challenge of our life is that these two aspects conflict with each other, mostly at the subconscious level. Thus begins a struggle in our lower mind where we move towards one and then because of something happening we change direction and head towards the other. Up and down, we go, repeatedly, never ever reaching our full potential. This becomes the dominant cycle of our lives... moving back and forth between heading for *Everything* and heading towards *Nothing*.

The model (as explained in *'Your Worthiness Cycle'*) has evolved over the past twenty years to be a way of understanding why everything happens, and then how to change this dynamic every time you are temped to run towards hell and away from Heaven.

The model is visual, so it *'shows'* you how to avoid the pitfalls and traps that stand in the way of your growth. It provides ways for you to 'up' your *'Worthiness quotient'* so you are able to attract and receive more of the good things in life rather than how to work harder, for less, which is how most of us do it, most of the time.

While there is actually no such thing as 'unworthiness', we all have blocks to our awareness of our true innocence and infinite value. Without an ability to access this on demand, we become unable to construct our life so that we gain more than we feel we are worth at that moment. Our deeply hidden belief, false as it is, is that we are not worthy of everything we desire, when we desire it, in abundance. The degree to which we can access our worthiness is what I call your 'Worthiness Quotient."

Without a new level of awareness, understanding and skills, our overall level of achievements will not rise much beyond where our highest point has been to date. Most people do, in fact, *'die with their music still in them.'*

Worthiness IS The Gateway to Everything

Almost twenty years ago I made these statements and nothing I have learned, since has changed my mind... in fact I feel even stronger today about what I said then:

> *"Worthiness is the most important thing you will ever learn about yourself and others."*
>
> *"Worthiness is the gateway to everything good that we desire in our lives."*

Why do I say that Worthiness helps me to Experience Mr. Zee?

- *Because I feel I have a good understanding of the holistic matrix in which we all live.*
- *Because I am willing and able to experience deeper and deeper levels within myself without 'losing myself.'*
- *Because I feel worthy of Mr. Zee's love and connection.*
- *Because I feel innocent enough to live most of the time without higher levels of guilt, shame or fear.*
- *Because I feel my value enough to be willing to receive the benefits of such an expansive and profound connection.*
- *Because I have cleared my mind enough to be willing to include more of 'The Truth' in my truth.*

I'm sure by now you are beginning to understand why Worthiness, as I explain it, is having a significant affect on, not only experiencing your loved ones returning from the Afterlife, and all other things metaphysical, but in every other aspect of your life as well.

On the next page are two visual representations of this life long cycle that I use to explain how to attain greater things in abundance. To learn more, you can access my book *'Your Worthiness Cycle'* available on Amazon and Worthiness.com.

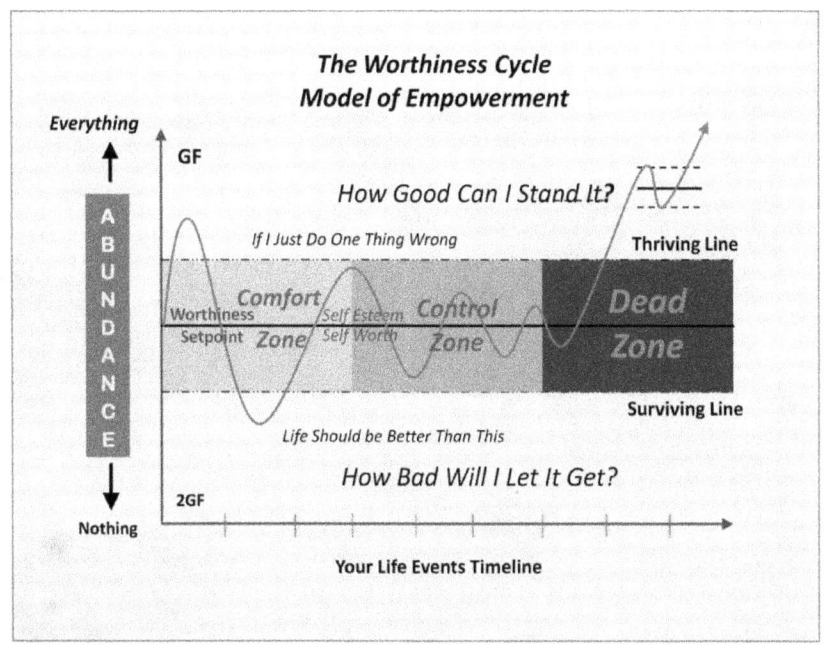

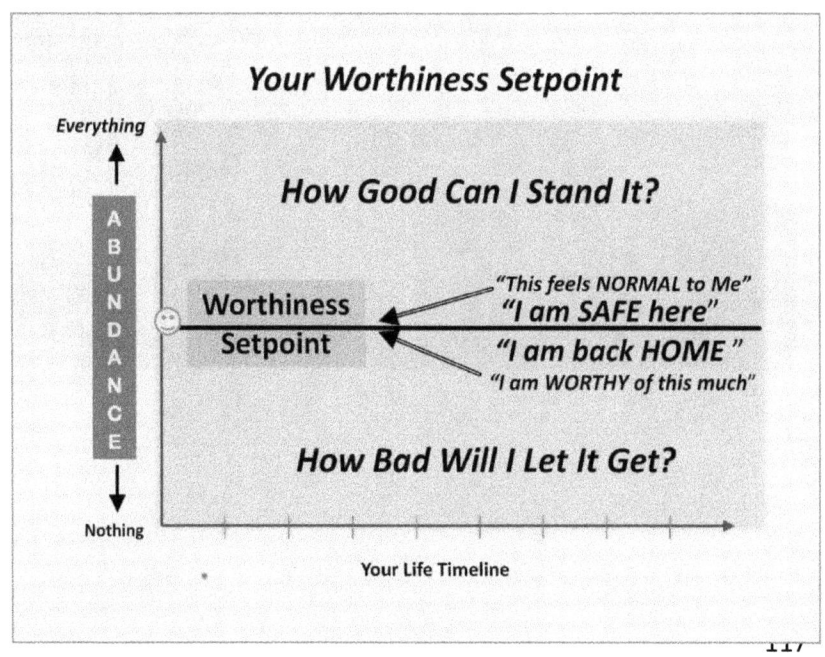

The body

is just a tool...

To enter into

the universe

which is the soul!

by Annabella

Stay Tuned. This Adventure Continues

> Any glimpse into the life of an animal quickens our own and makes it so much the larger and better in every way.
> ~ John Muir

In Conclusion (for now)

The visits continue to this day, although the frequency has subsided slightly. The routines have settled in, with minor modifications and changes in order and timing.

For now, I have decided to close this book. I plan to publish updates on a blog on the website as 'Mr. Zee and Company' perform more interesting and unusual things.

Although I never considered doing research into the paranormal I am exciting of the prospects and will report my findings and discoveries via the website and blog post articles.

Visit the Website MrZeeComesHome.com

Updates will be added to the website MrZeeComesHome.com and via Pawcasts.com

Today, on the website, you will find more links to others who have had the experience of their pet coming back. There are even some pictures on the website of 'ghost cats.'

What Have I Learned?

> "It is wonderful that five thousand years have now elapsed since the creation of the world, and still it is undecided whether or not there has ever been an instance of the spirit of any person appearing after death. All argument is against it; but all belief is for it.
> ~ SAMUEL JOHNSON, The Life of Samuel Johnson

Mr. Zee gave me a great gift, perhaps the greatest gift that can ever be given. He provided me with proof enough for me that **we do not die**. There is nothing new about that idea, but each of us has to discover the truth of it in our own time and our own way. I hope that this book has either assured you of what you already know or assisted you on your own journey towards this truth.

I have learned that we can communicate with loved ones who have passed over and that they are only ever a single thought or heart beat away from being with us, at our side.

I have learned that the energy of the Universe is a real thing and that it sustains us all without prejudice. It is our birthright and we need only to *get out of our own way* in order to receive it in as much abundance as we can stand at the time.

I firmly believe that Mr. Zee returned because of the deep bond we have. I love this cat as much as I have loved any person, animal or thing and that Love had somehow facilitated this incredible experience and all the life lessons that are available along with it.

I have learned that Love and Friendship is eternal and carries on with us when we leave this worldly dimension.

I have learned that I need to do nothing to be loved and feel deserving.

I have learned, and am remembering more easily all the time, that whatever the question, problem or challenge, Love is the only answer.

> *I wish I could show you when you are lonely or in darkness*
> *the astonishing light of your own being.*
> *~ Hafiz*

Hear These Words

A much-loved song says all of what I have wanted to convey in this book.

First written in 1966, this song was a number one hit for Marvin Gaye and Tammi Terrell, and then taken to the top again by Dianna Ross and the Supremes.

It has done nothing but grow in popularity ever since. On YouTube, which has only been around since 2005, it has had more than sixty million listens. It is as popular today as the day it was first released.

What is it about this song that reaches and reassures the deepest part of our inner most being?

I believe the lyrics are not just a love song. We can hear them spoken by many different people, who we want to know continue to love us, today, yesterday and for always.

> The words can be heard from lovers in our past.
>
> They can be the words we want to convey, but cannot.
>
> They can be heard as words of assurance from those we love who have died.
>
> They can be the words of our God, who wants us to hear them and know we are cherished unconditionally, no matter what.
>
> They can even be words of a crazy cat, who just wants his pal know that he lives on... and is only ever just a single thought away.

Hear these words. Let them reach deep into your heart and you will forever be with loved ones, pet or person, no matter where they are. Truly hear these words and you will never be lonely ever again...

> *If you need me, call me*
> *No matter where you are, no matter how far*
> *Just call my name; I'll be there in a hurry*
> *On that you can depend and never worry*
>
> *No wind, no rain, nor winters cold*
> *Can stop me, babe, Oh, baby...*
> *if you're my goal*
>
> *I know you must follow the sun*

Wherever it leads, but remember
If you should fall short of your desires
Remember life holds for you one guarantee
You'll always have me

You see, my love is alive
It's like a seed, that only needs the thought
of you to grow.
So if you feel the need for company,
Please, my darling, let it be me.

I may not be able to express the depth...
Of the love I feel for you... but a writer put it very nicely
When he was away from the one he loved.
He sat down and wrote these words:

No wind, no rain,
Nor winter's cold can stop me babe...
Oh, baby...
If you're my goal...

And if you should miss my love one of these old days,
If you should ever miss the arms that used to hold you so close,
Or the lips that used to touch you so tenderly
Just remember what I told you... the day I set you free

Ain't no mountain high enough
Ain't no valley low enough
Ain't no river wide enough
To keep me from you

Ain't no mountain high enough
Nothing can keep me, keep me from you!

Nothing in this world...can keep me from you babe!
Nothing... No thing can stop me now!

Appendix

Chronological Order of Events and Happening

Month / Year   Event

1973 - My Encounter at the House in Brandon.

1994 - Seeing an aura for the first time.

Spring 1998 - Zulu arrives.

Summer 2000 - Mr. Zee arrives.

Spring 2003 - Zulu dies.

Fall 2003 - Tanis and I go our separate ways. She gets the car. I get Mr. Zee.

July 2004 - Mr. Zee and I move into the Marpole area of Vancouver.

Spring 2006 - First bowel blockage

Spring 2010 - Second bowel blockage.

June 18, 2010 - Mr. Zee's death.

June 22, 2010 - The knock at the door.

June 24, 2010 - Letter to my friends about Mr. Zee dying.

July 05, 2010 - Published Eulogy on Facebook.

Mid July 2010 - First and second encounters.

Fall 2010 – Brief and sporadic encounters.

January 2011 - Move to Florida and then to Phoenix.

January 2013 - First major happenings.

Fall 2013 - Many visits in a row, at three different locations. I begin research in earnest.

September 2013 - First daytime visit.

My letter to friends and family on June 24, 2010

Dear Friends:

It is with much sadness that I report to you my friends that our beloved Mr. Zee has left us for higher places.

As many of you know he had been recovering from his seconded bowel blockage. He was gaining weight and was on the mend.

I awoke Saturday morning to realize he had not come home the night before. I worried that he had walked away, deciding to die on his own, but it didn't seem right to me in that he had been happy lately and we had become even closer as he allowed me to serve his daily medical needs.

I finally found out from one of the neighbors on Tuesday that they had witnessed him being killed by Coyotes.

I'm sure it was a fast death and he did not suffer but it still sends shudders down my spine when I think about it.

Mr. Zee came into my life when Tanis and I decided to get a friend for Miss Zulu. This was in 2000. We first saw him at a Petcetera store in Delta. Tanis said "he's he one" but when we returned he had been moved to "The Cat Lady's House" in Surrey where he was housed with 60 or so other cats up for adoption.

When we finally found him he was perched high up overlooking all the other cats and he had this funny grin on his face which I recognized right away. It said… "I am up here looking cool and smug but I'm actually scared out of my skin."(I knew the look well and knew we would be life-long friends as a result.)

When we brought him home Miss Zulu took one look at him and expelled half her hair. There was just this big pile of hair left, like she just had a major haircut. He wanted to cuddle with her right away but she would have none of it until a few years later when she was dying herself and Mr. Zee climbed up on the couch with her and wrapped himself around her. His redemption in her eyes was one of the last things she did and it meant a lot to all of us there at the time.

After Tanis and I went our separate ways I often joked that..."Tanis got the car and I got the cat... I got the better deal."

There are so many things that Mr. Zee and I went through together. To sum that up I would say that I woke up in so many ways while we were together. There were so very rough times where I had to decide who I was going to buy food for that day. I am proud that I made the decision I did. It showed me a whole new level of commitment that I needed to access within myself.

We were inseparable, as much as any cat can be inseparable with a mere human. I have a picture of one day where I was working on my computer and he put his head down on my arm. My mouse arm) and he just fell asleep. I grabbed my cell phone with the other hand and took an eye level picture without him waking up.

Mr. Zee had some funny quirks like all of us do. He loved to be petted but he didn't like his eyes or his paws touched. I tried and tried.

We had the same routine for many years. I would try to drop down for a nap around 4:30pm. He would somehow know that I had dropped to the couch and would instantly wake up, come to couch and jump up on me and flop down on my chest with he's eyes looking straight into mine.

First the left check just below the ear, then behind the ear, then same thing the other side, then under the chin and back of the head then down each side to the flank and back again. Finally after two years of trying he allowed me to rub his closed eyes with the back of my finger and he found out that was his favorite spot. Lately we had been working on the paws and the ever protected belly region and were almost there.

Often I would wake up after 30 minutes and he was still fast asleep. When he did awaken he would look deep and directly into my eyes and into my soul and connect with me like no other being on this planet has ever connected.

He always got hungry around 4am and would jump on the bed and prod me with his paw until I go up. When that didn't work he would jump over to the bedside table and swoosh off of it with his tail, anything that he thought I would get angry about (usually my glasses). Either way, whether it was noisy or valuable he always managed to perturb me enough to have his early breakfast meal.

In the last year or so he had taken to sleeping "on me" all night long. He would find a spot on me, a hip, a leg, the groin and he would lay down, give himself a bath, and then drop off, staying there the whole night. At first I would shoo him off but had given in lately, resigned to the idea that I was going to be his personal pillow for the duration.

After a while got used to it and for the past few days have been doing the widow's walk, pacing around in the middle of the night, trying to replace the warm, comfort and security he provided me throughout the night. It seems he was the pillow after all.

I am missing him very much for a long time. I learned so much from Mr. Z. I think we both had some karma to clean up and I'm sure we served each other well in that area.

I'm spending Sunday morning remembering him so if any of you would like to call or write with your memories you are most welcome to do so.

God Speed to you Mr. Z. It was an honor to know you and to serve you

Your pal for ever,
Allan

A Letter of Condolence from Tanis

Hello Allan,

I'm very sad to hear this news but I also recognized that Mr. Z's time to leave this planet was drawing near. We were both very blessed to be a part of his life. I will always remember the day we brought him home and yes... the high perch he stood on like a King when we arrived to pick him up.

For me he will always be the King of cats just as Miss Zulu was the ultimate cat Princess! These dear animals brought such joy to our lives... and "white" will always conjure thoughts and memories of two small creatures who enriched our lives when times were tough.

This is a painful loss for you Allan. I know how much you cared for Mr. Z. I hope that as time passes you will be comforted by the memories of the King cat who came to worship and adore you. Mr. Z was by your side through thick and thin. Please remember that you were also by his side.

Mr. Z was independent until age caught up with him... you allowed him to live with dignity and grace Allan with no expectations. He was ready to leave... I saw it in his eyes. I also saw trust and, despite his cruel death, the animal kingdom serves on many fronts.

I will take some time on Sunday to honor Mr. Zee and the gifts he gave to me. If I can provide some comfort for you Allan I would be happy to do so.

The circle of life is fascinating... I suspect that the King of cats is telling everyone in cat heaven that he got a pretty good deal.. just misses those moments of resting on the hand that fed him, loved him, fought with him and worried about him. Mr. Z would say that he was truly blessed to learn what love is thru you.

Now I will go and have my tears... Thank you Allan

Pets Coming Back Research

Here are a few of the results of the Google Searches I did the night I thought I was going bonkers. I searched 'My Pet is a Ghost' and 'My Cat Came Back after Death" stories. There are a few links to these stories. The url's to these and many more are on the website MrZeeComesHome.com

All stories remain the copyrighted owner of the original website they were first posted on and are provided here and on associated websites for research purposes only.

Our Cat Came Back to Visit Us After She Died
http://www.beliefnet.com/Love-Family/Pets/Feline-Angel.aspx

The Cat Came Back
http://www.catster.com/lifestyle/cat-ghost-visited-life-after-death

Haunted By My Dead Cat?
http://www.beyondreligion.com/su_personal/ADCs-cat.htm

A Cat Came Back
http://www.abovetopsecret.com/forum/thread821834/pg1

My Cat Came To Say Goodbye
What happens to our pets when they die?

Pictures of Cats That Have Appeared in Photographs

These pictures are off the Internet that resulted from a Google search in the Images section using the words 'ghost cat.'

I am sure that many of these pictures were captured by accident. Many of them are authentic but a few are hoaxes I am sure. I have done no investigation, as to which is which.

I have not modified the photos in any way other than to change them from color to black and white and to resize them to fit in the book format used for this book. The URL's have been provided below each picture and you can go to the website for easier access via your web browser.

All photographs remain the copyrighted owner of the original website they were first posted to and are provided here and on the associated websites for research purposes only.

Pictures of the paranormal have become much more possible since the advent of digital photography. A digital camera takes a picture of light spectrums beyond the ability of the human eye to see. Visit the websites for a more complete explanation of this and how to capture these types of pictures for yourself.

http://www.ghostalabama.com/Pictures/Ghost%20Cat%20cls%201.jpg

http://sparkyspitfire.wordpress.com/the-few-the-proud-the-felines-2/tom-civil-war-ghost-cat-also-dc-washington-dcs-kitteh-from-hell/

http://sevgilove.blogspot.ca/2010/10/ghost-cat-photos.html

MrZeeComesHome.com

Find our version of
Ain't No Mountain High Enough in the
Members section of the website.

Updates of the continuing adventures of
Mr. Zee along with new pictures, stories
and links are added regularly.

Join us in the Members Area and tell us about your
adventures with a pet that has made a return visit.

Please 'Like' us on Facebook at:
Facebook.com/mrzcomeshome

Thank You for Reviewing This Book on Amazon
http://bit.do/MrZeeReviews

www.ingramcontent.com/pod-product-compliance
Lightning Source LLC
Chambersburg PA
CBHW071517040426
42444CB00008B/1678